ON BELONGING:

reflections of a renegade guide

Saira Niazi

Dedicated to my mum and dad

Contents

Prologue 1

On Communication
Introduction 9
Writing 15
Photography 25
Storytelling 34
Conversations 36
Non-Verbal Communication 41

On Exploring
Introduction 44
Exploring to Learn 57
Exploring to Heal 61
Play 65
Commuting 73
Travel 80

On Unexpected Connections
Introduction 89
Wandering Connections 99
A Tooting Wandering 103
Patterns in Our Lives 104

On Faith
Introduction 111
The Stranger's Journey 113
Spaces and Faith 118
Safety 124
Struggle 126

On Transience
Introduction 130

Loneliness	133
Vulnerability	138
Goodbyes	142

On Love
Introduction	146
Romantic Love	149
Dating	152
Strange Love	157
Parental Love	159

On Being a Woman of Colour
Introduction	161
Gender	165
Guiding	170
Business	174
Power and Solidarity	176

On Community
Community	180

On Mental Health
Mental Health	192

On Privilege
Privilege	199

Epilogue 203

Acknowledgements 205

What you seek is seeking you — Rumi

Prologue

I'm sat on a ledge on a rooftop, watching as the sun sinks into a misty orange skyline punctuated with minarets, fruit trees, towering bird cages, and washing lines draped with colourful chadors. The sky is teeming with predatory black kites and a stray paper one too, it lurches erratically across the sky. The air is laden with sound; revving motorbikes, rickety rickshaws, bird song, noisy children. It's hard to place where the sounds are coming from. Below are a maze of gullies or lanes lined with small shops and houses.

As the sun disappears into the crowded horizon, a sense of peace, hard-fought-for, and difficult to hold on to, spreads through me and settles in my heart. It's strange how little seems to have changed since the last time I was in Lahore more than eight years ago and even further back, when I was a child.

Earlier on in the day, I revisited the local Baghbanpura bazaar with my mum. The bazaar, a great labyrinthine street market, colourful and frenetic, stretches across endless lanes and unlikely corners. As we wandered through the bazaar, we passed by countless stalls filled with all sorts of things; vegetables, clothes, stationery, books, rose petals, and dried apricots. Street food vendors flogged their samosas and chaats, chai walas weaved their way through the crowds with a tray of teacups in one hand and a thermos in another. As we approached the end of a lane, my eyes were drawn to a cage full of crows, a young girl handed a scruffy elder a hundred rupees to free one. He opened the cage and pulled out a bewildered black bird – after a moment's hesitation, it took off into the sky.

The adhaan began to sound out from a loudspeaker outside a masjid and men streamed out of hidden doors and narrow alleys for jummah prayers. It felt like everything was as it had always been – the same trader worked the same stall, only the creases on his face had become more pronounced and the circles under his eyes darker in colour. The same sad donkey carried the same heavy load on his back. The same gaggle of wool-dyed henna orange sheep sipped water from a trough on a roadside. The same children in their same uniforms walked the same lanes - the mystics, the nowhere boys, the women shrouded in chadors - every scene felt familiar. In my mind's eye, the bazaar had always been a place shrouded in mystery, of stories untold and connections manifest.

I remember my first visit so vividly. I was nine years old. My cousin Achi was planning to cycle to the market at night to meet his brother Vayd who ran a gold shop. Ever curious, I begged him to let me tag along. He relented finally. That night I hopped onto the back of his bike, and off we went. The markets felt dreamlike, busy stalls were lit up with hanging lightbulbs. On the way, my foot brushed against the wheel of the bicycle shedding the skin on its sole, rendering it bloodied. I never said a word, afraid that I'd get into trouble. It was only after we arrived at the market, I showed my cousin my injury. In a state of panic, he took me to a makeshift doctor's surgery somewhere in the folds of the market. A man with a very distinct mustache stuck a needle in my leg and bandaged up my foot. Soon after my uncle arrived to take me home. I did get into trouble, a lot of trouble. But that didn't stop me. A few weeks later, I found myself on the back of another cousins' motorbike on my way to visit a cricket ground. I've always been curious and one for adventures. I loved exploring as a child, and over the decades that love has grown and flourished in mysterious ways.

Once we got the odd bits we needed from the bazaar, mum and I wandered out of the markets and onto the busy dusty wondrous Grand Trunk Road. The ever-familiar technicolour trucks were parked on the roadside, alongside wooden carts stacked with symmetrical layers of oranges and apples. We bought some fruit from a vendor and walked to Shalamar Gardens where we settled on the grass to have a picnic. The beautiful Mughal gardens looked the same, only the fountains weren't running; the waters had run dry. Once we finished our picnic, we began to wander back and my mum pointed out the fruit trees that surrounded us – the tall mangos, spindly oranges, cowering guavas. I felt my soul exhale. I had so many happy memories of the faded beautiful grounds. During my last visit, my dad and I would often set off at dawn and walk to the gardens from our home. Home - a place I once lived and came to deeply love, a place I had finally, after so many years, returned to.

My mum and I are back in the house my grandfather had built - two women from two different generations belonging to two different worlds, together for a time, learning from each other, listening, and trying to understand. It is here I find myself asking, what does it mean to belong? Growing up, my parents always told us we would soon go back "home," and naively I believed them, as they believed themselves. I spent my childhood and teenage years in a state of mental transit, never here nor there. I'd keep a cardboard box filled with items to take with me – odd bits and pieces, paintings, letters and notebooks filled with childish dreams.

There were a few occasions we made real attempts to relocate. When my grandmother became very ill, my mum pulled my sisters and me out of school and we came to Lahore where we lived together for four months. We'd spend our time playing in the garden my grandfather looked after, seeking shade under mango trees and pomegranate trees. My sister and I took entrance exams at a local school. My grandfather and uncle built us a house. Time went by so slowly, a month went by, then another, and another and another. My grandmother passed away and finally, my dad called us back to London. It was so difficult to leave, to say goodbye – it always is.

I've longed for a time I could arrive in Lahore to stay, to not have to say goodbye – that too sorrowful word that has forever haunted my life and relationships. It always lingers in the air, like a dark cloud, our impending departures. I've become so accustomed to getting close to others, only to leave them behind or vice versa. I have longed to find a place I can feel anchored to+, yet find peace in the freedom of being unattached to people and places. Maybe this is one of the reasons I've always been so fascinated by notions of belonging, home, and connection.

Often, as children of first-generation immigrants, you live fragmented lives and you yourself begin to fragment and leave essential parts of yourself in the places you tarry, in return you carry with you, essential parts of others' – their stories, the places that bind you together. You begin to recognize the privileges and adversities that come with being the 'other,' you realise that geographically and culturally you belong nowhere and that nowhere can be a place of power as much as of displacement. It forces us to look inwards. In doing so, we realise the truth, that we belong to ourselves; we find meaning in our own narrative, in the miracles, patterns, and events that grace our lives rendering them unique and multifaceted. But more essentially, we belong to God.

In many ways, Lahore is where my journey towards becoming a renegade guide began. Eight years ago, I spent the better part of three months exploring and playing guide to my wondrous little cousins, we'd hike in jungles, visit the beautiful mosques and bustling markets, traverse open fields and play in ancient gardens. Although I was a stranger to the city in so many ways, struggling often to communicate and to truly understand, I wanted to explore and to instill within those around me the value of exploration. I drew out lessons that could be learned on our journeys. I encouraged my cousins to share their thoughts and ideas. I sought always to evoke within them a sense of fascination and pride in the city they called home. Back then, I went through some very dark episodes. There were times I felt like my world was aflame, that my beliefs were obsolete, and life had no meaning – but what saved me? My explorations - everyday observations that reminded me that life was so much bigger than I thought it to be, that the possibilities are endless, to connect to other humans, and to feel that connection was enough.

There are so many things I loved and valued in Lahore, coming from a family whose members are spread across continents, I found it so novel and beautiful to be able to create rich friendships with elders and children, to teach and learn and to love and be loved. I've always had a volatile relationship with Lahore, my ancestral motherland. It's a beautiful paradoxical city, where epiphanies appear in abundance and the actualization of them a rarity. It's a place that forces you to confront yourself, it's a place where love is bountiful, and family is a word laden with meaning - duty, warmth, loyalty, and kindness. It is also a place, that as a woman, can often render you small, vulnerable, and stuck.

Lahore never fails to teach and reteach me the value of freedom, in a city in which I often felt so suffocated and restricted. I often return to London with a renewed sense of appreciation for the city I was born in, a city that has afforded me great freedom, independence, and opportunity. London – a city I love and know so well, a city where I have found a way to make a living as a renegade guide.

Following our trip to the bazaar and Shalamar Gardens, we received some visitors – my cousins. The boys had become little men, inches, facial hair and deepened voices were indicators that although for me the last eight years had been a blur, time had pushed on. The girls had become little women. It's a bittersweet feeling, coming back to a place, and feeling a sense of disconnection to people you were once so close to. One of my cousins, Polli, was only twelve years old when I was last in Lahore. He was now taller than me. He had the same mischievous dancing eyes. "You haven't changed at all!" he exclaimed in Punjabi at the end of our conversation when we were first reunited. I smiled and nodded, but deep down I knew that I had changed, beyond belief, and so had he.

You have to pay attention to notice change. Often change is subtle and difficult to decipher. The roads are a little neater. The rubbish tip at the end of the road where the cows would graze no longer exists. Local parks which were mostly frequented by drug dealers are now enjoyed by families. The orange train line is almost complete. New gated communities have popped up in areas further afield. The social fabric of communal and familial life has in some ways, begun to unravel.

It feels darker now, light is less apparent, but maybe it's because it's winter and I'm looking in the wrong places. Many of my relatives have grown older and wearier. It feels as though every household has been afflicted in some way - unemployment, black magic, poor health, abusive neighbours, familial burdens, financial stress. Their problems make me feel so small and so helpless and so shamefully privileged. My call for action has remained the same - go for a wander, observe, learn, and heal through your observations. Seek out new frontiers in your city - collect stories, show kindness, find freedom and peace in the wonderment of every day, and in helping others where they are struggling.

The answer here in Lahore feels so naïve, childish, and empty, but also permitting. To physically remove yourself from a situation for a while, to get out of your own head, and to be in the world; to wander - it is a source of healing. Is my work purposeful? I often find myself asking this question. In the face of struggle – of collective adversity, a far-reaching malaise, great and deep, and made all the worse by fear – does my work feel empty in this place? What does it really mean to be a guide? Why did I choose this path, of all the paths that I saw stretched out before me?

It's only upon returning to Lahore, after so much has passed and having changed course innumerable times, having lost and found myself in the dark and light, and having continued to search, always, for new ways to live in peace, that I realise that so much of who I am, the decisions I have made and the life I lead is owing to the stretches of time I spent in Lahore.

Upon finding myself lost and alone, I found within me the desire to guide others the way I wish I had been guided. Perhaps it's owing to a lasting sense of dislocation (both spatial and cultural) that I became a renegade guide, and in turn, realized the value of being shown a way or a multitude of ways.

People are so strange and wondrous, filled with ideas and stories and possibilities, to be able to draw these out is a privilege and a blessing. I like to make people feel welcomed and happy, often to be more than a guide for a fleeting time - to be a friend, a well-wisher, someone who listens. I love the synchronicity that graces each wandering, the unexpected encounters, and uncanny connections. I love the wonder, mystery, transience, sorrow, joy, healing, and alchemy that comes with being a guide. Embarking on this journey, I have learnt to invert my emotions – to create space for others when I feel constricted, to listen when I want to be heard, to inspire when I feel nothing, and to instill in others a sense of belonging, at times when I feel most distant.

Returning to Lahore hasn't been easy, it's marked the slow and quiet burning away of a multitude of dreams I've held close to my heart, but perhaps their embers will give light and life to new dreams. I believe it was my kismet to return to Lahore and to write a book that is meaningful to me – a book about my journey towards becoming a guide and how this role has influenced my character, deepened my faith, shaped my life, and changed the way I view the world.

February 2020

On Communication

He (Musa) said: "O my Lord! Open for me my chest. And ease my task for me; And loosen the knot from my tongue, that they understand my speech." — The Quran

I'm sat typing on my laptop by the balcony of my room in Lahore in a dusty echoic empty house. I can hear the birds chirping outside and the recitation of a naat sounding out from a speaker. A naat is a devotional melodic song expressing a love for God. It's beautiful and calming, though I can't understand the words, I can feel them. The reciter's voice is filled with hope and sorrow and hurt and love, the emotions travel from his heart, they escape his lips and reverberate through the air for everyone in the gully to hear: the children playing on rooftops above, the women putting out their laundry, the cleaners sweeping the streets below. He is communicating, through song, he is reaching souls who may be open to receiving.

    I didn't bring my phone to Lahore - no Instagram, no Twitter, no WhatsApp, no Spotify, no notifications, in many ways I'm cut off, rendered quiet for the first time in a very long while. I thought I would feel alone and isolated, but instead, I feel so much peace and gratitude. I'm grateful to have time and space to myself, to be able to disengage and not communicate.

    When I was a child, I couldn't easily express myself. There were a lot of words I couldn't pronounce properly. I would say choilet instead of toilet, sometimes I would say things in the wrong order, and I wouldn't make sense at all. I saw a speech therapist occasionally with whom I would carry out activities. She would use pictorial aids to help me to say things better. Maybe it was for this reason, I was a quiet child. I went on to be a quiet teenager. I didn't have many friends. I was never one to put my hand up in class and hated it when teachers picked on me. On a few occasions, my dad would ask my teacher during Parents Evening if I was being bullied (much to my horror) since I didn't talk much at home either. I remember in Year 11, my Media Studies teacher, Mr. Meade, once told me I was the most dejected student he had ever taught. I later looked up what dejected meant; miserable, dispirited. I found it funny but in a sad way because I didn't see myself as being dejected. I felt misunderstood and I felt frustrated that I was never truly able to express myself eloquently in ways that I wished that I could have.

I painted and read. I spent a lot of time in the library and I imagined, wrote, and wandered and found other ways to express myself. I would often bunk off school and seek solace in places where I could be alone and quiet without being admonished for it; mostly green spaces, nowhere spaces like cemeteries, but also large crowded places where I could feel anonymous, like markets and museums. I had an avid sense of adventure and loved embarking on solo expeditions. During my teenage years, whenever I had time off, I got the tube (at that time, a day travelcard only cost one pound if you were under sixteen) to random places, and sometimes I'd meet random people and share random conversations.

On my last day of school, I went to the park and set my uniform on fire. For a brief while I felt free, the future felt wide open. When I started college, a good hour away from home, I was presented with the opportunity to recreate myself. I didn't have to be cripplingly shy, or withdrawn or quiet – I could be myself. I longed to be myself, and I knew myself as being someone who had a lot to say. College was worse than school. I didn't fit in. I couldn't connect. I began failing all of my classes.

I went through a dark year-long period of depression. I felt small and inadequate and cursed, more than that, I felt lonely. When I wasn't in class, I spent much of my time by the river in Richmond nearby my college. I sought solace in writing and wandering and watching the world, sometimes engaging with it, though it felt cold and so did all the people in it.

It was during this time I wrote my first book, Freegan Freedom, a novel that explored the relationships between a group of dissimilar Londoners living in an abandoned building brought together by fate and connected through a shared anti-materialistic and communitarian ethos.

The protagonist of the story was a young man named Sebastian. At the age of fifteen, he finds himself living on the streets of a dark and surreal London. One unlikely day he meets a quirky beatnik who leads him through a labyrinth into his inimitable world, a world in which ten dissimilar freegans are living together in an abandoned building. Sebastian soon adopts their freegan traits and finds a place within the strange family unit. Three years later his feelings of dissatisfaction resurface. He struggles to deal with his own lack of direction, feelings of alienation and childhood deprivation as he goes on an unforgettable journey of self-discovery. The journey begins when he finds a friend in an unlikely companion; an offbeat Muslim girl who challenges stereotypes in many shapes and forms.

In some ways, writing helped me to forget myself and to explore notions of identity and ways of life. It also offered me a sense of escapism, which I craved desperately. I lived in my book, I spent time with the characters in it and at various points in my life, I found the characters and stories manifested. I encountered them in the material world, in some form or another. The book became a part of my life and my story, but at the time of writing it, I couldn't shake the feeling of sadness.

It took a myriad of things to take me out of that dark place including a renewing trip to Lahore, to the mountains of Murree, and the hills of Kashmir. Trips to the motherland have always acted as a catalyst to some great inner and outer change. I emerged with a whole new sense of perspective and self, rooted in gratitude. I decided to let go and to use my energy to give back. I volunteered as a playworker at a school in Brixton and at a refugee and asylum seeker drop-in centre. I made an effort to love more, to lose the separation that had become part of my identity, and to allow myself to be part of a community or multiple communities. I also made a friend; a Korean art student named Chanmi who I met through Gumtree. She had put up an ad on a language exchange forum that I was interested in taking part in. We met and got on like a house of fire. Finally, I found someone I could be myself with. It felt like we were soulmates, a decade on we still share the same connection. She taught me the value of true friendship among so many other things.

    I also began to learn sign language and undertook courses at a local community college for two years. I was fascinated by this nonverbal form of communication; the beauty, and power it held. At the time, I wasn't sure why I wanted to learn British Sign Language but it helped a lot when I became a community worker, working with elders and as a guide, learning to decipher the needs and expressions of individuals who spoke little or no English. It was during my multiple trips to Lahore that I became interested in ways in which to communicate without words - how do you communicate acceptance and love and kindness? Smiles became valuable lingual currency as did embraces, grimaces, and reassuring pats.

    In my early twenties, I underwent a spiritual journey. Quietness as an inferior personality trait was no longer a truth I subscribed to. I saw it as a powerful tool through which I could communicate with God. I began to learn how to listen to myself and observe the signs around me. I gave myself permission to be quiet. I would often embark on long hikes alone and stay in hostels during which time I would utter a few words in days. I would walk through fields at sunrise and watch the sheep. I realized then why so many prophets were shepherds. I would recite scriptures, Quranic verses, and engage in dhikr (remembrance). I found respite in quiet and being quiet. It's something I've carried with me throughout my life – a need at times, to be alone and quiet, in and among nature - to be mindful.

I've always been an introvert; curious, quiet, and with a passion for creating and for communicating. My first few graduate jobs (ironically) were in communications and public relations. I've worked countless jobs, each very different from the last until I became a guide. I find it so strange that I became a guide - someone who talks in front of crowds of people. Possessing an almost aphasia, it's taken forever and a day to learn how to speak eloquently, to communicate in a way that is engaging and coherent – a way that is fitting of a guide – to form connections and build bridges through words.

To this day I still struggle to communicate. I often speak too fast, and stumble over my words and forget them completely or pronounce them wrong. I remember on one occasion saying to a group "you'll often see peasants wandering in the cemetery" – of course, I meant to say pheasants. I got some confused looks before self-correcting and laughing at myself, thereby permitting others to laugh at me too. I guess the older you get, the less self-conscious you become. I felt like I had something to say. And my need to share was greater than my need to possess a certain level of decorum. My sisters say that I speak my own language, some kind of post-communication dialect whereby I string random words together and hope people will understand – it's a language borne out of frustration. When your mouth can't keep up with your mind, everything comes out in a beautiful incoherent jumble.

I've always had an interest in language and our ability and inability to express ourselves, often finding most tools to be lacking and rudimentary and never allowing for true expression, however the beauty is in the attempt, and it's something I've never given up on.

Writing

"The world of reality has its limits; the world of imagination is boundless" — Jean Jacque Rousseau

"Aap writer ho bhaji Saira?" Are you a writer sister Saira? My cousin Hajji asked me this question last night upon seeing my stacks of notebooks and a pile of pens. I said yes. For the first time in my life, I said yes, and I said yes with a self-assurance and relief that I had not felt or expressed before.

I'm a writer. For as long as I've known, I have written. I have written letters and articles, diaries, and journals. I've written hundreds of poems. I've written short stories and novels. I'm writing this book. It's what I've always dreamed of becoming but have never given myself permission to be – to lay claim to the title and to believe it, truly. Much of what I've written remains unshared. I have a bookshelf filled with books I've written, books I've self-published, and placed on my shelf for no one to read but myself. Why? Because I love writing, I love speaking in similes and metaphors, expressing myself in ways I often can't through verbal communication. I love writing in colours. I write because I enjoy turning experiences around, slowly in the light.

I write to capture and preserve valuable stories. I write because there is a need within me to write. My writings bind and liberate me, render me vulnerable - render me, me. My writing provides me with lessons and epiphanies. In the folds of each manuscript, I find miracles, clarity, and inspiration. Writing enables me to remember that which I am sure to forget, small details - like the hues of black that make up the crow perched on a thick wire stretched across the balcony behind the large veiled window of my writer's room. He is gazing down onto the street, at the rickshaws and residents that pass through.

Writing allows me to explore and imagine the connections between people and place, inspired by the things I see and find on my wanderings. I once unexpectedly came by a white chattri, a war memorial for Indian soldiers who had died in the Second World War, in the Sussex countryside. Many months later, I was inspired to write a story about a lonely and homesick Indian student, Sunil, who found a sense of home at the chattri. He had been befriended by a guru named Sri Navaganshi by the sea in Brighton and following a long conversation about displacement and belonging, the guru had taken him up to the chattri. It had since become Sunil's safe space, he'd hike up at night, light incense, and lie on the steps of the chattri staring at the stars, thinking about his village back home, his family, his hollowed dreams. He would hear the whispers of the soldiers who died in a land so far from home and he felt a sense of comfort. The universe has a way of bringing people into our lives, unexpectedly – meaningfully. Not long after I finished writing the story, I met a professor, he was a writer too, half Indian, who had a guru of his own. I shared the story with him and in return, he shared some of his writings. The connections you create through words and stories run deep.

I wrote many short stories about the South Downs. A lone wander in Eastbourne inspired a story about a teenage boy named Tyrone, from Stockwell, who after being suspended from class found himself on a train to an unknown seaside town, and then gravitating towards the green hills. He settles on a patch on the top of a hill and reflects on the day's events and the run-up to them, all of which are contributing to the disintegration of his life - gang involvement, familial obligations, lack of physical and mental space, urban decay and a sense that his destiny would be bleak. Whilst ruminating, Tyrone is pulled out of his thoughts and into the present by the murmur of starlings that drift together across the sky – for a brief while, he is rendered free. He no longer feels constricted, mentally or physically – instead, he feels, for the first time, a sense of possibility, of space, and peace. He feels a sense of belonging with the land so far removed from the urban cityscapes he's used to. And so it is with writing. Writing fills us with perspective and gratitude and a sense of connection.

    I was sat by a dew pond under a windswept tree contemplating life one afternoon on the Downs, not far from Seaford. I was inspired to write a story about a dying woman named Edna and her connection to that very dew pond. In the story, it was a space she had frequented since childhood, seeking refuge there whenever she felt a heaviness, a sense of desperation, fear, or loneliness. On one visit, as she felt death drawing closer to her, Edna looked into the dew pond and found that it had become a watery screen through which she was able to see her life played back to her; every epiphany, every heartbreak, every dream, every weighty and life-changing moment, whimsy and wonder, came and disappeared. She cried and she cried; her teardrops fell into the water and she felt herself become part of the pond. She walked back down to her home, feeling consoled and resolved in herself. She felt her faith had returned to itself.

    A trip to Westfields on Boxing Day, a traumatizing experience in and of itself, lent inspiration for a monologue piece on an Eastend woman who is martyred in Forever 21 by a crowd of shoppers. As a pointed railing goes through her and those around her continue to madly search for cheap deals, she (in a humorous but sad way) talks about the absurdity of it all; consumerism and greed – resulting in her bloodied end and the fact that it has all led to her now about to die in Forever 21.

On the platform of a suburban railway station, a friend and I met a butler named Bill. He called himself "The White Jeffrey" (in homage to a character from 90s sitcom 'The Fresh Prince of Bel-Air'), and enjoyed a good curry at the Regents Park mosque café. The encounter lent itself to a story. An unlikely encounter with a stranger at the job centre turns a depressing visit into an exercise of curiosity; the beginnings of a story, and stories give life – they allow you to transmute experiences, find magic in the mundane.

I love writing poems - playful poems, inspired by my observations. Mr. Bean on the central line train sews a button onto his blazer. A busker sings a song I only ever heard in a dream. A homeless man shares a prophecy. Three fabulously dressed elderly women have a giggle at the bus shelter. An elderly West Indian man wearing a top hat plays his saxophone in a tree. A bird watcher spends the morning in the Peacock tower, still and silent and searching for an old feathered friend... the light seeps through the cracks in the heavy grey sky spelling out an emotion not yet named. I love watching the world, watching people, and creating scenarios, dialogues and my own endings.

I've written the most whilst working jobs that have allowed for prolonged periods of people-watching, jobs in places including museums and nature reserves. They're brilliant and sometimes maddening places to watch and to wonder, to be present and absent – and to learn about the human condition. Many of my poems were born out of boredom and frustration, sometimes out of pain, sometimes out of joy and curiosity and wonder – to live in between the real world and the world of imagination, of dreams, has been a refuge and a compensation.

I've wandered for as long as I've written, over the years I've wandered for endless miles, traversing spaces both mundane and sacred - the house of dreams, secret gardens, colourful studios, crypts and caves, bingo halls and bus garages, derelict factories, disused reservoirs, mosques and temples and churches, and synagogues - thousands of places. I've wandered by day and night, penning my explorations, my insights, and the stories I've unearthed on my journeys. During my explorations, I've met all sorts of interesting and extraordinary human beings - nuns, monks, poets, activists, artists, storytellers, inventors, ex-offenders, and fellow wanderers. I've connected with communities of West Indian and Nepalese and Irish elders with the rich and varied life stories, and with youth who have already lived out several divergent versions of life. I've found endless inspiration on the streets - often the stories I've come by in real life have been far stranger and more wondrous than those I've conjured up in my imagination.

I wrote over a hundred and sixty thousand words on the real-life encounters, observations, explorations, and stories I've come by on my countless wanderings across the city. I dreamed of turning it into a book, a book on a Living London, on the communities, individuals, and spaces that render the city so marvelous, and multilayered and strange and interesting - so unlike anywhere else in the world. It became, in part, a historical archive, a visual and written documentation of the places that no longer exist and the stories that surround them.

My wanderings have turned me into a storyteller, and I share my writings through the retelling of stories of the people I meet and, sometimes, the direction they point me in. A tracker of killer animals turned nature reserve manager who resembles a Viking tells me to keep knocking on doors - to never give up. A lighthouse keeper who looks like a businessman introduces me to an inventor who resides in a hut by the waterside. A mudlark who collects letters in bottles shares a particularly moving message she found inside one. You learn to suspend your disbelief and your judgements, nothing is as it seems – no one is as they seem, there are mystics within us all.

I never finished writing my book, Living London. It lies buried in a folder among other unfinished works. I decided to write this one instead - perhaps it is more befitting and whole. To communicate at your own pace and in your own way through the written word has always felt powerful beyond measure. Writing is a gift, it allows for regeneration, it allows you to capture emotions and experiences before you begin to remember them differently or cease to remember them at all.

I've had bits published; articles on secret spaces, on material wonderlands and makers' spaces, and on secret wanderings. I've recalled certain more memorable wanderings - like a dawn walk in Walworth – plasters strewn across the concrete, neon signs in foggy darkness, a fading Elephant, soon to be lost forever. I've shared insights on the changes, the disappearing landmarks, the extraordinary people and community projects – the soon-to-be demolished Elephant and Castle shopping centre, the bathhouse that used to be a Buddhist temple, the community canteen, the church crypt where people sought shelter during the blitz, the high street that giraffes once traversed in the middle of the night. Writing has allowed me to share the knowledge that has taken me my whole life to acquire, knowledge that I've come by in unlikely and unexpected ways.

As with most things, there's a synchronicity that marks your journey when you're on the right track. You meet the people that you need to meet, people that will help you to grow, kindred spirits, in this context, other writers. To be a writer, it is a difficult undertaking that often yields little reward in terms of security and financial gain. But writing is life-affirming and restorative, and often worth the struggle.

As I got off a train at Clapham Junction, a lady called out in my direction– yoo-hoo! She waved at me. She had a waiflike frame and silver hair down to her shoulders. I vaguely recognized her. She was in my pottery class. I waved back and we exchanged a few pleasantries. The next time I attended pottery class, she sat next to me and we talked about all sorts of creative and interesting things. I was eighteen at the time, she looked like she was possibly in her sixties, but possessed a youthful air about her. Her name was Chris, she was at the time undertaking a PhD in Greek Tragedy. She was a mask maker, an artist, a theatre practitioner, a writer - and soon became my friend, supporter, and in some ways, guru. Over the next ten years, we embarked on countless wanderings across London, seeking out special places, playing with paint and ink, and sharing our creative works - our art, our writing. She had so many interesting stories, having spent her early life in El Salvador with her parents, both of whom were very different from each other. I got to know her husband too. He was a very polite and very spirited economist. The three of us would often engage in long rambling conversations in Chris' artist studio. They both encouraged my creativity, in particular my writing. Chris always pushed me to continue down the creative path I had by default found myself on, however difficult it may be.

Over the years, I've met and developed friendships with writers from many backgrounds who have inspired me beyond belief, and often these encounters have been so unlikely and enlightening. I met a Colombian writer, Juan, who had also worked as a guide in New York. He had more stories than I could imagine - stories of mostly walking from Colombia to the Amazon rainforest in his younger years. I met a talented and soulful Somali poet, Samra, whose words on home and love and loss, move me. A scriptwriter, Fatuma, who writes beautiful stories from the fringes of society.

I once met an author and artist on the internet who went on to become an unlikely pen pal. He was older than I was, and our lives were immensely different. He was divorced and had children. We shared our short stories and ideas that emerged from our writings. He was from up north and shared a passion for many of the same things that I did. We met once when he was in London for the day for a television interview about his newest book. We met in Chinatown, the setting of his first book. We spent the day wandering around London under the sun, talking as we went, he felt like an old friend – not a stranger. We wandered by the river, and by the book market at the Southbank, we wandered into St Paul's cathedral, it was Ash Wednesday – the light was beautiful. At the end of our walk, we said goodbye. I never met him again, and eventually, our friendship came to an end. We both shared valuable learnings. His way of life, his confidence in his writing, and his path as a creative gave me hope. In some ways, I felt a kinship with him.

My writing has connected me to so many different people, guides who have helped me to grow. One day I came across a project online called '5 am London'. It was run by a woman named Gemma. One morning at 5 am, she received an anonymous text which read 'I don't know when I'll be home.' She lay awake wondering who might have sent the message. In the following months, she would explore the city at 5 am seeking traces of the person who sent it and others like them. Gemma's work fascinated me. After doing a bit of digging, I found out she ran early morning creative writing workshops. We met and decided to collaborate. I would lead a sunrise wandering and she would provide writing prompts.

During our first collaborative walk, we gathered a group of writers at dawn and we wandered through London. We wandered through the deserted graffiti tunnel, and down picturesque Roupell Street with its Victorian workers' cottages and iconic chimneys. We wandered down to the river foreshore, the sun was rising, the morning light was magnificent and the writers wrote by the shore – we were bound together through our love of writing, a passion that found us awake and exploring, in a sleepless city, seeking inspiration in stories. We wandered through patches of green, towards a secret community garden, before ending with a breakfast picnic by the river looking out onto Tower Bridge.

A year later, we collaborated again one spring morning. Many of the same writers came along. We wandered through Chelsea, passing by colourful streets, and the Royal Hospital for Pensioners, and Chelsea Physic Garden, then wandered across the glorious Albert Bridge. The light was again magnificent, and the streets were so quiet. We wandered through Battersea Park, seeking out nature in the deserted Herb Garden before ending with a breakfast in the beautiful Old English Garden. The fountain was shooting up water in the ornamental pond in the centre and the garden was beginning to bloom - colours abounded. I met a lot of people on that walk. On most of the walks I've been on, there's been one person that has stood out to me, and they've stayed in my memory over the following years, even though I had met them only once. That morning, it was a writer who seemed slightly otherworldly. I think he was of North African heritage. He was working on a book and would spend most of his time in the London Library. He would sleep for only three hours a night and embark on wanderings while the city was in deep slumber. I felt a sense of unspoken comradery with him, with all the writers, who seemed to drift in and out of their own secret worlds. As a guide, I've become so used to meeting people, sharing deep conversations, then never seeing or hearing from them again, and that in itself is quite beautiful. Transience and intangibility are themes that have remained throughout my life and are reflected in my works.

A few of my closest friendships are long-distance friendships - maintained sporadically through the written word. We write letters to each other- long thought-out letters, sharing our innermost thoughts and feelings, across oceans. One of my best friends, Rahel, moved to her motherland of Turkey not long after we met almost a decade ago at university - we consequently, over the years become close friends, and to this day we write each other letters. Our friendship has always felt somewhat elusive - we meet for short periods whenever Rahel finds herself in London. She is a magical human being, a writer, photographer, and filmmaker - we have so much in common. During her infrequent visits, we would find ourselves wandering, by waterways in Hackney and through the streets of Southbank - rambling on and on, having so much to say but little time to say it all in. Our goodbyes were always premature; a prologue, an interlude, and an epilogue. We would open up to each other about our struggles with mental health, creativity, faith, film - and despite the distance, through writing, we remain close to each other.

Writing is magic. It connects you to others. It opens you to new worlds, ideas, communities, and experiences. You can live a hundred lives and meet hundreds of people, without leaving the same place. It is a refuge, a place to reside, a place to imagine and dream. In a world in which the dreamer is often admonished for being childish and unrealistic, it is an unreachable retreat. I turned thirty not so long ago, and conversations around me are more and more turning to marriage, children, careers, property, and titles - all of which, still, much to my detriment perhaps, seem irrelevant to my life's journey. Here in Lahore, I often feel dismissed or insignificant for not ascribing to a way of life deemed normal or ordinary. I wonder if the very act of writing this book, to those around me, seems pitiful - but I write and I write and I write.

On Photography

"My life is shaped by the urgent need to wander and observe, and my camera is my passport." — Steve McCurry

I didn't bring my camera with me to Lahore this time. It was a difficult decision to make, to leave it behind. I've had a camera since I was fifteen. I love taking pictures. At various points in my life, I have attempted to make a living as a photographer.

When I was in college, I dropped out of photography in my first few weeks because I couldn't afford a camera. My education maintenance grant had been stopped and I used the money from my weekend job as a pharmacy assistant to pay for train fares to Richmond. I didn't receive formal training or a decent camera for a very long time. God often brings you back to the things that you love in mysterious ways.

A day before I flew out to Lahore on my previous trip eight years ago, I went to Argos and bought three large boxes of Duracell batteries for my cheap second-hand Olympus camera. Although I didn't have a plan for what I would be doing in Lahore, I knew that I would be taking a lot of pictures. I've always been interested in photography and the powerful role images can play in challenging views, changing perceptions, and facilitating change. Over the years prior I had worked on various photography projects all of which sought to override shallow and reductive representations of certain places and peoples.

When I first arrived in Lahore on my last visit I half expected to be met by angry mobs, explosions, and hordes of dengue mosquitoes on the prowl. The reality of life (in Lahore at least) was not so dramatic or menacing. During my three months of working and living in Lahore, I discovered a new Pakistan, one which often remains hidden from the public eye. It is a beautiful Pakistan filled with colour, magic, and intrigue. Despite all its problems, to me, Pakistan remains one of the most interesting places in the world. I found the people living there to be incredibly sincere, generous, and spirited. This is what I wanted to capture through my photography. I wanted to take pictures that depicted the true reality of everyday life in the city. I wanted to capture images that told stories and truthfully conveyed the essence of the people I met.

What struck me was the resourcefulness of the people of Lahore. Rarely did I come across someone begging, rather one would always have a service on offer - one man would be selling balloons, another mending pots on the side road, a few children would gather shoes to shine. The people made the best of what they were given - they worked hard to receive the little they got.

I also wanted to capture the colour and the mysticism of Lahore, for all the stereotypes perpetuated of Pakistan as a dark, dangerous and violent country, I found the city to be a very colourful place. From soft pastels to garish neons, colour was to be found everywhere - on buses, trucks, markets, people's clothes, decorations, even the graves, this to me reflected the qualities I found in many of the Lahori people I came to meet. A side that presented a certain creativity, humour, playfulness.

I took a lot of pictures of children. I believe that wherever you go in the world, children are by and large the same. They love to play and laugh and to cause mischief. Children remind us of how we used to be, back before we became aware of our differences, before we formed ideas and identities often rooted in our insecurities and fears. They remind us of simpler times, and I believe if we let them, they can inspire us to recreate those simpler times - that sense of freedom and exploration.

When I returned to London, I put on a photography exhibition in Brixton Village. One of my images received a special mention and was exhibited in the Mica Gallery in Chelsea. To this day, I have mixed feelings about displaying the photographs I took, they were so sacred and special to me – they represented real connections and secret stories. Although my intentions were good, it didn't feel right. To be entrusted by a stranger to take their photograph is a privilege and it comes with a lot of responsibility.

In some ways, photography not only allowed me to communicate through images, but it also paved the way for communication. With a camera in my hand and a smile on my face, I found it easier to start conversations, to talk to people in broken Urdu, to get out of my head, and to understand. It lay down the foundations for me to carry out similar projects in different cities, in Busan and Sydney. Photography took me out of myself. Especially during the times I found myself wandering alone. As with writing, I take photographs because it brings me joy, because it allows for expression.

A few years after my return to London, I won a DSLR camera in a competition run by Time Out and the Media Trust. To enter you had to submit a photograph that expressed what London meant to you together with some words on the image. I was at the time working in conservation and was obsessed with ethereal and ancient green spaces. The photograph I submitted was of my friend Shaun, a conservation land officer at the London Wildlife Trust, gazing at a gravestone in Nunhead cemetery on one of our wanderings. I wrote about the timeless sacredness of London's secret wild spaces.

As part of the prize, I got to meet and talk to the staff photographer at Time Out London, Rob Grieg. He offered me advice and insights into the world of London photography. In the years that followed, I took my camera everywhere I went. I took it to work and on my wanderings. I took thousands of photos of secret spaces and strangers on the streets. I took on photography projects which involved working with communities across London. My favorite project later evolved into a film about Nepalese migrant women and their connection to home through song. It was largely filmed at a community garden in Plumstead called Bostall Gardens where the women, mostly elders, would grow food.

In London, wandering alone as I mostly did, I was able to hide behind my camera lens. My camera would, as in Lahore, make it easier for me to connect with others. A windmill photographer lent me his fish-eye lens at Brixton Windmill. He pointed out a parhelion, a broken bit of rainbow in the sky and retold stories of all the windmills he'd photographed around the country. Whilst working on a story about the gentrification of Tooting Markets, I spoke to many stallholders at Broadway Market. At the end of our conversations, I took their photographs in their space, that would then go on to be featured in Huck Magazine. Together with words, I felt the images told a fuller story.

I've also curated an exhibition of some of my favourite hidden London gems and stories. It took place in a former fishmonger in Poplar and it marked the end (and in some ways the beginning) of the Living London project. On the white walls, were excerpts from my book in progress together with photographs of places so dissimilar: a mosque, a museum, an eco-squat, a crystal cave. Each picture told a story. I love taking photographs of desolate spaces, urban and wild - chapel ruins, deserted hills - perhaps it reflects the sense of aloneness that has characterized much of my work and wanderings.

Once I was walking in Jangsan mountain in Busan, South Korea. I was acutely aware of all the things I should have been afraid of whilst hiking up a small nameless path – there were warning signs of landmines, the sun was sinking, I was completely lost. I remember then, stumbling across a house and some chickens in the yard. I could hear a song playing from the yard, a song I'd sung a hundred times. The words danced in the air around me: *twenty-five years and my life is still, trying to get up that great big hill of hope... for a destination.* I remember laughing to myself at the strangeness of life. Soon enough my anxiety and fear returned, it was my camera that kept me going. It gave me something to focus on. I was practicing the art of looking, searching, for something beautiful and worthy of remembrance – to be in a moment and capture it forever. To take yourself out of a situation for a moment - a brief moment – is invaluable.

    I experienced similar moments whilst wandering alone in the Bushland in the outskirts of Sydney. Whenever I heard a rustle, or thought of a snake or coming across someone who might be dangerous, I would pause and take a photograph. It was a meditation. It made me forget myself, and observe everything everywhere, the small details – the patterns of the rocks, the glistening waters below, the marks on the bark of a gum tree and eucalyptus tree.

    I took a lot of photographs while I was in Busan for some months. It would make my lone wanderings more purposeful. I'd walk different routes and take photos of the everyday magic that I found in unlikely places. Of fragile encounters I watched unfurl; an elderly lady flogging fish, a couple wandering by the beach, a beatnik busker singing Simon and Garfunkel's "Sound of Silence", whilst on a late-night walk, a man taking out his binoculars to search for birds. The excitement of capturing something real and beautiful brings about a deep joy. I love photography. I've worked with film and digital, I enjoy playing with images, preserving memories, refiguring them, distorting them, turning them into something else entirely.

Often on my tours, I'll use pictures as prompts as they can be read by anyone, and in different ways. I always encourage people to bring a camera on a wandering and I'm always so fascinated by what they choose to capture.

I once led a wandering for a group of photographers from the Instagrammers London community. The walk was along the river Wandle – we visited the remains of a historic Chapter House and the former site of William Morris' printing workshop. We visited Abbey Mills, a waterwheel and pottery house and animal farm, and wetlands, before ending at Morden Hall Park, a pretty National Trust site. It was the slowest walk I had ever led. It made me see the trail, one I'd walked a hundred times over, differently. Each capture and perspective was unique. The outcome of the wandering encapsulated various ways of seeing. The diversity of the pictures reflected the diversity of the group itself. Every individual I spoke to on the walk was so interesting. I met a photographer named Julia who was born and grew up in Siberia. I met a kind, creative and spiritual Mauritian named Imran. Everyone had their reason for coming on the walk, and for being drawn to the art of photography. The walk marked the beginning of many lasting friendships.

I've connected with various photography communities since - I love that most people take photographs because it's what they love to do, what they're passionate about. I've met so many talented, funny, authentic Londoners – each quite obsessive about their practice and the city they call home. Many of them would chase sunsets and sunrises. I felt a kinship with them and I discovered new ways of seeing. Photography in some ways, allows you to take ownership of your city – to capture it in a way that is true to you.

I met and conversed with many photographers that inspired me over the years. I met the rooftop photographer James Burns, we share an affinity for high places and the

English weather. Over the last decade, he has captured a changing London skyline from the rooftops of buildings like Centrepoint and Grenfell Tower and Trellick Tower. He has a wealth of stories. He's taken wondrous iconic photographs of London from above, in lightning storms and fog, a rainbow, a full moon. I met the City at Dawn photographer Anthony Epes, known for taking photographs, remote and lonely, of cities at dawn. I once attended his City at Dawn London workshop, the meeting place was the middle of Waterloo Bridge, at 4am on a summer's day. It was ghostly quiet, a group of us gathered - sleepy-eyed but excited. I was the only female in the group. Most of the men lugged around heavy expensive photography gear. We traversed all sorts of dissimilar spaces, taking photographs as the sun began to rise.

There have been so many photography projects that I've found so interesting. Joshua Blackburn's "Launderama" - he photographed every launderette in the city. Each launderette depicts a story. I remember I wanted to do a similar project many years prior when I made friends with an elder who ran a launderette in my area – an Iranian named Sam, who survived two bouts of cancer and still worked the machines. He used to be a naval officer. His children no longer come to see him. Every space is filled with stories.

My favourite London photographers are those who capture stories from the fringes through photography - they tell stories of the communities that are often ignored - capturing tender moments, against an urban background. I love the work of my friend Sana Badri – her images communicate authentic connection and the joy and beauty of every day. She captures the richness and complexities of diverse London. London, a city forever in flux, where old and new are never far apart, where often identity can be fluid, social, racial and class boundaries blur, and people connect and come together in unlikely spaces.

Photography allows for connection amongst photographers too. It's a way of asserting a sense of belonging. I was once involved with a collective called Off Centre, it was a photography network run by three inspiring British Bengali Muslims, Salman, Ibrahim, and Redhwan. It aimed to create a community and to allow young POC creatives the space and support to connect, to traverse spaces, spaces often not seen to be 'theirs', and to lay claim to them. I found the project to be so inspiring to me personally - having spent most of my youth exploring alone with my camera and often having to be brazen enough to cross boundaries (physical and mental) alone. I saw value in what they were doing. I wished that the community existed when I was younger. On one of their walks, over fifty people attended with their digital SLRS, phone cameras, and drones. We wandered through Hampstead Heath and the Pergola Gardens, everyone was talking and taking photographs and exploring and playing. It was beautiful. The walk ended at twilight on the summit of Primrose Hill, the group broke apart and many stayed on to pray under the stars.

As a renegade guide, I've learnt to be innovative and to do things differently – to generate ideas that inspire and provide opportunities for others and an income for me. I once had a meeting with a lady named Lizzy, a manager of a beautiful hotel. It was previously a town hall and was filled with stories of love and loss. The hotel itself was grand and beautiful and full of character. I had the idea of running a photography competition, through which photographers would be invited into this space to capture all that made it unique. It was nice to invite the public into a five-star hotel and for them to explore, wander, and capture it. At the end of the day, participants were asked to upload their captures onto Instagram with a hashtag, to be judged. I've always had a slight aversion to social media, in particular Instagram, a channel which breeds vanity and where your work is judged by the number of likes received. It's not a space in which I feel my photography has been seen – maybe there aren't many people interested in seeing pictures of a clown church or crematorium, as much as there are wanting to see a stylish woman against a pretty backdrop or the London skyline from the Shard. But as photographers, we do what we do out of love.

*

I thought it would be difficult and frustrating to be in Lahore without my camera, there was always so much to capture. But it's been so easy, it's taken the pressure off and allowed me to take things in with my eyes - a horse wandering down the road at midnight, the smoke-filled gully, the faithful returning from the masjid at dawn break. It makes me feel more present, less restless, and more in tune with my surroundings. I'm part of the world, not looking at it through a lens. There's more room for intangibility, for memories shrouded in unreality, for peace.

Storytelling

"Many stories matter. Stories have been used to dispossess and to malign. But stories can also be used to empower, and to humanize. Stories can break the dignity of a people. But stories can also repair that broken dignity." — Chimamanda Ngozi Adichie

Storytelling allows you to bring images and words to life through speech - in ways that seek to evoke emotion, to inspire, illuminate, and inform.

I tell a lot of stories on my wandering tours. I have collected over a thousand and will often share one whenever it feels right or relevant. I share my own stories, my own experiences of the places we visit on a wandering tour, stories of the people, and the communities that make the spaces so special. My wandering tours are often unscripted allowing me to elaborate, extend, pick the stories that most suit the people I'm exploring with, pick the projects and places that are meaningful to them. You can withhold or share as many details as you like.

In truth, I've sometimes felt a bit uncomfortable sharing stories. I try to be as accurate as I can and to share only that which I deem worthy or interesting or inspiring. I sometimes wonder, who am I to share this story - beautiful, sacred, not mine? The aim of my explorations was never really to share the stories I came by. They emerged not through interviews but through genuine interactions, through sincerely talking to the people that I met. Conversations arose out of curiosity - a willingness to listen, to talk, and to reveal.

Maybe this is why I will never complete and share that book, Living London. To go back, and find all the people I met, to ask their permission to share their photos and stories, would be a mammoth task, and it would change the nature of the very project. But to share fragments, namelessly and in ways that might illuminate others in the ways they illuminated me, is so valuable. Intentions are integral to all the things we do as artists. To be truthful and authentic in what we do and in what we put forward is so important. Sharing fragments of life as a way to connect people to the present and themselves, has always acted as a catalyst for those on the receiving end to reveal stories and insights of their own. The wanderings allow room for dialogue, for more stories to be shared and for further opportunities to learn and connect. Each walk with a group of strangers becomes something greater in and of itself, a shared and intimate experience.

Conversations

"If there's any kind of magic in this world it must be in the attempt of understanding someone sharing something. I know, it's almost impossible to succeed but who cares really? The answer must be in the attempt." — Céline, Before Sunrise

Guiding often allows for two-way communication, more so if you're leading a private tour for an individual or small group. I love talking to people, especially people who are interesting and live a very different life from my own. I love learning. Being a guide, you often meet people from all walks of life. I've wandered with a Jewish doctor and theatre enthusiast from Jaffa who specialized in researching hallucinogenic drugs and had lived in places around the world. I've wandered with a young Danish Berber who after working seven years as a businessman quit to travel the world. I've wandered with a Brazilian journalist, a Uruguayan Professor, an Iranian war photographer, a South African teacher, a Singaporean personal assistant, a Black American nurse, a student from Saudi Arabia, Swedish entrepreneurs, Georgian mountain dwellers. I've wandered with aristocrats, filmmakers, actors. As a guide, you never know who you will meet, what they'll share with you, and what role they'll come to play in your life, if any, and it's this possibility that keeps drawing me back to guiding.

During the tours you can talk about things that have meaning, you can ask big questions and answer big questions, on life, love, on dreams and politics and religion. You learn and you share. It is an exchange and sometimes it's difficult, and the answers don't come easily and you're challenged in mysterious ways. Sometimes your answers change, your answers to questions about your dreams and desires - sometimes they stay the same. Sometimes your answers surprise you when questioned on deeply personal things like whether or not you believe in soulmates, whether or not you'll ever write that book, or take that trip that you've talked about forever. Often it's those that you feel you'll have the least in common with, that you in fact have the most to talk about. It's the private wanderings tours that I often find more memorable, individuals let down their guard and let you in.

Sometimes a few words with a stranger can mark the beginning of a lasting friendship. I once met a young lady named Cherin on an island by the sea in Busan. I was going for my daily walk when she appeared from nowhere. She asked if she could take my photograph and I said yes. I asked if I could take her photograph too. She was beautiful. It was a brief but uplifting encounter. Two souls coming together, it felt like we shared the same energy – wandering women with our cameras hanging from our necks.

The next day we met again at the same place by chance, and we ended up spending the entire day together. We talked about music, about James Blake and Lindisfarne, we talked about art, and travel and writing and photography. We had everything in common, two drifting dreamers. Like me, she took her notebook and camera everywhere she went. That day we wandered by the beach, and into a photography gallery, we sat in a café together, had lunch in a hotel, and watched the sunset by the marina. We became friends. I introduced her to Chanmi, my best friend, and whose sofa I had been sleeping on throughout winter. Together the three of us shared many happy memories, we listened to jazz and enjoyed feasts on Chanmi's shabby boat. A year on from the day Cherin and I met, the three of us were reunited in Paris. We spent the night wandering through the picturesque moonlit streets of Montmartre talking about everything and being silent too.

Over the years I've led hundreds of wanderings in areas across London, for those visiting the city and those who know it well, for strangers and friends. I've led walks for elders and students, for groups of businessmen and women, for hotel staff, for writers and photographers, for families – the way I communicate, the way we relate to each other is often so revealing and unique. As a guide, you're forced to adapt, to be fluid and versatile. One day you find yourself with a group in Claridge's in Mayfair, wearing your smartest coat, standing a bit taller and talking a bit posher, the next you're with a group of teenagers from south London in Southwark. It's a job that requires emotional intelligence, but also the ability to converse and relate to anyone – no matter how different you perceive them to be, no matter what their background.

Sometimes conversations don't come easily, especially when those you're leading a tour for speak limited or no English. How can I communicate this in a way that you may understand? The answer changes in any given situation. I once led a tour for a group of mostly French Moroccan men. They brought with them their translator. It was a very nerve-wracking experience, having to form more simple and coherent sentences when I had only mastered the art of rambling. I hoped the translator translated properly. Outside one of our stops, one of the guests in the group pulled out his phone, and began using google translate. He said something in Arabic and it translated: **I AM VERY HAPPY. I WILL COME TO LONDON AGAIN WITH MY FAMILY.** I smiled, delighted. In these situations, smiles and laughs are of enormous value. When the tour ended, we all went for a meal at a Turkish restaurant under a mosque. I got a few friends to join us for a sort of cultural exchange. Members of the group asked questions about what it's like to be a British Muslim and about everyday life in London and we did our best to answer, we talked, we laughed, we understood and misunderstood each other and we ate.

Being able to communicate, especially whilst being lost in translation for pronounced periods of time, is so special. I once met a Pakistani labourer on the beach in South Korea. Somehow he knew I was Pakistani. We shared a few words in broken Urdu. I asked him if he knew where I could buy halal chicken. He led me to a market and then to a Punjabi restaurant. He paid a worker to bring me frozen chicken thighs. I thanked him and when I tried to repay him, he refused. I thanked him again and hesitantly went my own way. It was my first day wandering alone in Busan. I was truly grateful for his kindness. I wondered how lonely it must be, to be in pardes (a foreign land) so far from home. I prayed for him.

Conversations often lead to serendipitous encounters. Many years ago, I once had a strange dream. I dreamt that I walked to Lahore. When I awoke, I was sure this was my kismet and made a promise to myself, that I would walk to Lahore when I was thirty years old. (How fast time passes!) That very day, I visited Crossbones, an unconsecrated burial ground for the outcast dead – the resting place of paupers and prostitutes that had been transformed into a moving and mystical garden of remembrance. I got talking to a volunteer and somehow ended up telling her about my dream and desire to walk to my motherland. She said there was another woman, Sara, who had made a similar deal with her grandmother. She had promised her half-jokingly that if she were unmarried at thirty she would walk to Tehran via the river Thames and a myriad of other waterways. The volunteer gave me her email address and upon returning home, I wrote to her. A while later she replied, telling me she was preparing for the journey. She had mapped out the distances and received funding. A part of me was overjoyed and relieved that she was going through with it. Maybe it was enough and meant that I didn't have to. We planned to meet, but it never happened. I don't know if she ever did make it to Tehran. I never walked to Lahore, but I got here.

Non-Verbal Communication

"I closed my mouth and spoke to you in a hundred silent ways" — Rumi

There have been times where I've often had to translate and try to understand the words of those whose first language is not English. I've watched people struggle in frustration to communicate something and it's a frustration that I am well accustomed to. On my wanderings, I encourage people to speak, because I know how empowering it is to be able to communicate, but equally, I emphasize, often to their relief, that it's okay to be silent.

We communicate through art and objects, the things we put forward, and the things we leave behind. A colourful house that tells the life story of its owner. A religious effigy reveals the secrets behind a faith. We communicate using maps and symbols and silence.

I believe the most powerful form of communication is silence and that often, words aren't necessary. Speaking less enables you to see more, to truly observe and to take things in, things we miss whilst talking. I've spent the better part of days in shared silence with individuals that I've met through chance encounters, often whilst alone overseas. It's a beautiful thing to be able to remain largely silent: to point at things, to use your facial expressions to express yourself, and to use prompts and sign language. One day in Busan, I was wandering in the rain, two schoolgirls were wandering behind me, and one of them placed an umbrella over my head. They invited me to join them on a visit to the aquarium where they were headed. I agreed, grateful, and happy. During our time together, we talked a bit and laughed a bit but mostly we were quiet, we'd point at sharks and jellyfish and we took pictures together and we said goodbye.

Often on my tours, there are pronounced moments of silence, sometimes it's an easy silence and sometimes it isn't. Often there's less talking in a cemetery or a library. There's always welcome silence in a mosque or church or temple. We share a holy silence with God. A silence that heals, a silence in which we can hear ourselves finally - things come to us, divine wisdom, solutions to problems we never voice. I have a special place in my heart for those I can be silent with. In a world that is so noisy, where everyone seems to talk so much and say so little, I have learnt to appreciate silence and those who I can be silent with – the child within me, that socially awkward wordless child, exhales.

It has been there always. Silence. It is my oldest and truest friend. On many of my wanderings, silence has accompanied me, protected me, silence has shown me love and mercy, it's given me space to breathe. Silence is accepting, forbearing, it doesn't render you small and stupid like words do. The older I get, the more I come to appreciate silence.

*

Last night a few of my cousins came over. It's strange, they came over to speak to my mum and me. I don't think I'd ever been so quiet and lost for words or unwilling or unable to share anything of worth. The eldest, a handsome, religious, and very wise young man, was just a boy when I was last in Lahore. I'd always known him to be quiet and reserved, tonight he talked for what felt like a few hours. He shared religious wisdom and his views on politics. He shared stories of his childhood and the stories of people in his neighbourhood. He even talked about David Icke and Richard Branson. He talked about giving back and how fitnah (unrest) is widespread. He talked about piles of rubbish and dengue mosquitos. He talked about the selfishness of others. He talked about the water shortage and the storms battering the shores of England.

I stayed quiet throughout. There were a few times when I wanted to say something, but I didn't. The few things I did say, sounded childish and inane. My other two cousins and my mum engaged fully in the conversation. I felt a bit like I did when I was a child, socially awkward, and as though my tongue had been swallowed up. But at the same time, I felt a sense of calm. When they left, I didn't feel angry or ashamed of myself as I might have in the past. Though I wondered if they thought of me as a stupid privileged foreign brat. I hadn't been able to show them my real self. And it was okay. It felt like I had made progress. I did however feel exhausted and as though I had taken in far too much information. My cousins left, my male cousin Ali, didn't acknowledge me or say goodbye upon leaving. It reminded me that communication is so specific and so censored – often we don't get to choose who we talk to or how, especially when you're a young single woman visiting Lahore with your mum after a very long time. I felt small and unseen.

My voice sounds different in Urdu and Punjabi. It sounds high pitched and very feminine, for this reason, I used to hate speaking in Urdu. I felt like I didn't sound like myself. It was easy for others to speak over me, or dismiss me, everything that came out of my mouth sounded unimportant. When I was angry and tried to express myself in Urdu, I came off as screechy and unhinged. It rendered me powerless and frustrated. I've also never been able to articulate myself in the way I like. Often I silently congratulate myself when I'm coherent. Can I be myself whilst speaking a language that is quite unfamiliar to me? I am learning.

On Exploring

"We shall not cease from exploration, and the end of all our exploring will be to arrive where we started and know the place for the first time." — T.S. Eliot

This morning I visited Lahore Fort with my two female cousins and my mum. As part of the Lahore Art Biennale, the shadowy ancient ruins were filled with contemporary art created by Lahori artists – sculptures, and mixed media, stop-frame animations; wondrous images, and ethereal sounds surrounded us. As we wandered, we looked at the art and we looked at the people. There were many trendy art students around, dressed in quirky outfits, hair bleached. Everything seemed surreal. Maybe it was the neon or the cool air, or the fat raindrops falling from the elusive overcast sky outside, but I felt entirely elsewhere.

In Australia, I once took a ferry alone to Cockatoo Island to see some art. As part of the Sydney Art Biennale, the island had been transformed by artists. The sun was shining down on the island, a former prison/convict penal establishment, that had been mainly used as a place of secondary punishment for convicts who had re-offended in the colonies. The island was eerie, and there was a darkness to it. I wandered around the large open structures, each one was filled with noise and colour. Ideas had manifested into otherworldly works – there was so much to see. I wandered around for hours. It was a scorching hot day, the island was relatively quiet and I felt in equal parts free and alone.

This was during a month I spent in Australia, mostly wandering by myself in the bushland and by the coast. I'd often hike down from a suburb called Berowra, a word meaning 'a place of many shells' to Berowra Waters tucked deep in the Berowra Creek valley. I'd carry around a bottle of water and trail mix in my bag, sometimes a book. I'd take a nap on a rock under a gum tree. I'd rarely see other people. My brother and his wife lived in Berowra. They were mostly busy and I didn't mind the solitude. Often I'd take a ferry from Sydney Harbour to some random destination and just wander around. Sometimes I would write, the sun shone most days and the days were warm, although it was winter (for some reason I mostly only ever go away in winter). The nights would draw in early. Sometimes I'd walk under the moon over Sydney Harbour Bridge, by Luna Park; a ghostly quiet illuminated theme park. I'd wander in the diverse areas that reminded me of my hometown Tooting, in Auburn and Lukemba and Stratfield. I travelled to Melbourne. It rained almost every day while I was there. I'd seek shelter in markets and mosques, in gardens and libraries, and by the beach. I felt aimless. As ever, and with most of the trips I've been on, I didn't have a plan. I booked my flight just a week before I left London. It was a lonely time, but so freeing. In many ways, I was running away. I'd just had my heart broken and it had only been a few months since I had returned from Busan. I had nothing and no one anchoring me to any place. I needed space and physical freedom which I equated with an internal quietude. I sought consolation in my wanderings and through conversations I shared with God.

    I think that's the most difficult thing about being here in Lahore; the lack of freedom. I'm reminded that the freedom I've been afforded my whole life is a privilege and a blessing. Wandering is a blessing. Where I'm staying, and have stayed before many times, is a neighbourhood called Begumpura just off the Grand Trunk Road. Our house is tucked in the middle of a small road lined with sweet shops and corner shops. When I was a child, I begged my mum to let me go and get sweets with my cousins and she always refused, there were too many stories: stories of pedophiles, and crooks that would cut off the arms and legs of children and force them to beg on the streets, of old witches who would put them in sacks. My cousin once claimed someone tried to abduct her. She ran away. Coupled with other stories of jinns and robbers, it's no surprise that I didn't kick up too much of a fuss, especially as a child.

Those kinds of stories stay with you, they occupy the dark crevices of your heart and soul. It's a fear that never fully goes away. Only the fears evolve and transmute, nowadays I worry vaguely, more about the voyeuristic eyes of men. Too often I've been followed. Maybe people watch too much TV here, maybe people are lonely and looking for a love story like the ones in popular Pakistani dramas. It's more the fears of my mother I worry about. It's just my mum and me living in this vacant shadow-filled house. The walls are thin and noises are constant - of gunshots and revving motorbikes. She never sleeps. There's always the fear: of armed robbery, of creatures of the dark - ghouls and demons, addicts, and the desperate. Many of the stories come from a place of truth. My aunt who lives a few blocks down experienced a robbery, they tied members of the family to chairs, held them at gunpoint, and stole anything they could get their hands on. Still, if it weren't for my mother and her peace of mind, then I would roam freely.

Since I can't go for a wander here alone, sometimes I go for a wander in my mind around my grandparents' garden with its mango trees, guava trees, pomegranate trees, and reaching grapevines. My sisters and I would play in the mud when we were kids, among rabbits and creepy crawlies. It no longer exists - the garden. In my mind, I wander to the graveyard where my grandparents are buried. To my uncle's factory, now derelict. He passed too. I'd wander down nameless gullies, observing the faces of the children and elders that passed me by, the stray dog and stray cow sifting through piles of rubbish looking for something to eat. Sometimes I go for a wander in my mind, and I find myself in places dark in nature.

It feels strange to articulate it to my cousins, a gnawing frustration rooted in spending much time at home and only being able to leave the house with my mum. I get it. In the past, I put up such a fight to challenge superstitions and negativity. I got a job in Lahore, travelled around, I was even on GEO TV, a Pakistani television channel. I caused my mum a lot of stress. Our relatives would talk – they would say unkind things that perhaps possessed truth, like I was naïve and wild and jhalli (a foolish fickle girl). I felt restless and suffocated. I felt like I was constantly at war, fighting for my freedom.

I've changed a lot since then. I no longer feel the need to prove anything. Women work, they go to university, they're pushing for justice and equality. They're living their lives. I saw a young woman wandering in the zoo by herself the other day. It made me happy. I continue to speak out for women's rights but in a more subdued manner. On a personal level, I have become more accepting of my current situation. I came to Lahore for my mum, out of love and duty, but also out of curiosity and a deep desire to reconnect to the people, places, and dreams I left behind.

I've become calmer. I stay quiet, even when it's difficult. Maybe I've just grown tired or lost a bit of fight in me. Or maybe I'm embracing the fact that my journeying has to be inwards, and isn't that why I came here? To look inside myself, to write and to rest, and to spend time with my mother and with God. I know that when I return, I will be out again, walking again, guiding again, exploring and talking, summer is around the corner and it will probably be very busy. Maybe I'm learning that it's okay to be still sometimes – I'm learning to no longer avoid being with myself, but to listen to that inner voice, it becomes louder and clearer each passing dawn I spend alone wandering on the rooftop. I'm learning to not always seek out distractions and peace outside of myself.

When I went back to London eight years ago, I embraced my freedom as fully as I knew how. I went for long walks on the common and in the countryside, and I felt so much gratitude and awareness, and guilt. I've always felt a sense of guilt that I haven't yet resolved. I travelled a lot, to many countries – I relished in exploring. I've always hated being indoors. When I was young I developed a habit of walking and it was a habit encouraged by my dad.

I take after my dad in so many ways. He always wanted to work in the Pakistani railways as a child and when he was eighteen his dream manifested. He loved exploring, he'd get free train tickets and, when he wasn't working, we would explore Pakistan. My dad was different, he was extraordinary. He constantly struggled to live a life that was bigger than he knew. He grew up in a poor household, his dad and his brothers were all farmers. He was the only boy in his family who went to school. He went to a boarding school away from his village. He developed strong friendships but always felt disconnected from his family. He walked and cycled and he loved adventures.

It was this sense of adventure and exploration that took him to London. He had studied English, and he wanted a life of his own, a new life. He felt the possibilities would be greater and that the streets would be paved with gold. It wasn't how he imagined at all. It was a difficult lonely slog. Often my dad wonders whether it was the right decision, would he have been happier if he stayed in his homeland and built a life there? I always reassure him that it was the right decision, and that all of our lives would be infinitely more ordinary had he never left. In fact, my sisters and I would never have been more (but that's another story). Everything happens for a reason.

My dad has always been measured and free-thinking. He encouraged us to explore, and to work very hard, and to carve out our own paths. The freedom of choice he gave us, was always empowering, but also paralyzing. There were always so many choices, so many possibilities, and so many pathways. My dad switched jobs every few years. He tried out so many different things. He worked in a radio factory and as an accountant. He opened a restaurant with his best friend.

He experienced the kind of failures, disappointments, and utter heartbreaks that would make anyone give up, but he never did. He never gave up when he lost his beautiful beloved wife (years before meeting my mother), when he lost his job or when his children moved away. He was always resilient and strong and taught us to be the same, to have grit, to have faith, to forgive, to love, and to retain a sense of positivity and a sense of humour throughout.

Growing up, on weekends, it didn't matter how tired he was he would always take us places, to the South Downs, a fruit farm, to Brighton, to museums and to the park. He taught us to ride bikes and never let us feel like disappointments – however far off track we were from being conventionally successful. He always took our side when it came to us wanting to go off on our own, whether that was to Norfolk for a few weeks of quiet or to Korea for a few months of soul searching. This was quite rare for Pakistanis of my parents' generation. I don't think I realised how much courage it took for them to go against the grain. I've appreciated it always and promised myself that if I ever have children, to learn from my parents' ways. My dad has always been my greatest inspiration. The stories of our parents are so much richer and more layered than ours ever will be.

My dad and my mum have always been socially conscious, they have always taught us to do good by our neighbours, to work for our communities. I've carried these teachings with me wherever I've gone. I've always tried to include my parents in my endeavours. When I worked at the

Natural History Museum, and the Victoria and Albert Museum, The Wetland Centre, I would welcome them into these spaces and explore with them. As a community worker, I've shared with them countless stories of the people I work with, elders, those in crisis, those living on the streets or in the lonely dark spaces inside of themselves. I'd ask them for their advice and try to follow it. As a guide, I would involve them in projects, often oral history projects. I was once commissioned to create memory tours using the memories of Pakistani elders. As part of the project, I connected with a group of Pakistani women. One day I took my mum to meet them all in Cricklewood. I think for once she wasn't embarrassed of me being a guide. She felt included and relevant, the women made my mum feel like a sister and a friend. In coming to Lahore with my mum, exploring has become an emblem of self-empowerment that has deeply connected us both. My mum regales her sisters of our tales of when we're out alone in Lahore. It brings me great joy and peace in seeing her embrace her independence fully for the first time.

It's strange, my name, Saira, in Urdu means "Sair karne wali", "phirne wali" which literally means traveler or wandering bird. Saira means free soul, someone who traverses spaces and learns from these experiences. I only learnt the meaning of my name in recent years. I can't quite remember who mentioned it, but I remember looking it up afterwards on Google and feeling quite humbled and in awe of the fact that my character was so true to my name. What's in a name? Our souls.

I guess given my love for wandering and exploration, coupled with my interest in stories, it isn't so unusual that I became a guide. For me, guiding allowed me to share my learnings, stories and knowledge. Knowledge that I acquired over a period of ten years, and painstakingly recorded, gathered, and archived. It offered me an opportunity to, for the first time, make money from my work. It took me a while to realise that it was work, and it was of value. Although making money was never my motivation, it is integral to the continuity of my journey as a guide. The transition of turning my passion into my livelihood has been a difficult one and has taken many years of perseverance. I've quit jobs, given up opportunities, and sacrificed so much to keep guiding and carry on down the path I began treading. Sometimes I wonder if it's worth it. Some days, when it's really cold out, and I'm waiting for strangers to show up, and I'm feeling especially anti-social and low on energy, and I'm thinking about all that I've given to simply show up - those days I wonder if it's worth it. Deep down I know it is. It has to be. For me, one of the greatest motivators is to maintain a community that's emerged from this project - a project founded primarily on solitude, often isolation.

My early wanderings across London led me to unusual places — from burial grounds and bus garages to sewage works and costume stores. I got on night buses to nowhere, hiked through remote edgelands, among broken ships, mudflats, and heaps of trash. I explored abandoned factories, desolate lakes, and deserted museums, searched for treasure along the foreshore of the Thames at sunrise, and counted planes taking off from Heathrow runways at twilight. I tarried in temples and churches, mosques and synagogues — sometimes seeking home, but mostly just seeking a place to be for a while. On my journeys I met and befriended a multitude of interesting characters and came by all sorts of beautiful sights, a sixteen-hundred-year-old olive tree stump from Aleppo in an industrial yard, a kingfisher darting across a river beside a little known pathway, a man painting a wondrous mural.

I've learnt so much about the city and myself through my explorations, through unearthing secret spaces and talking to the strangers that render them so special. I love exploring. The reward is in the very act of exploration.

I've been fortunate enough to explore with friends – brilliant, inspiring, open friends, the kind that you can laugh endlessly with and share uncanny experiences with. One such friend, Halima, was a constant source of inspiration and consolation. We regularly embarked on adventures together, we'd wander by day and by night – crossing boundaries, geographical and otherwise. Our wanderings were often unplanned and always renewing.

More often than not, I've explored alone. Exploring alone allows you to go at your own pace, to go whenever you please. It renders you more open to your surroundings and allows for new connections to come about. You're more present. You can focus on where you are, take photos for as long as you like, take a brief nap, watch the world endlessly, be inspired to pen a poem. I've penned a lot of poems in a lot of places pertaining to a lot of people. Time flies when you're on your own. You can film the butterflies and the planes taking off, you can count them as they pass over your head. You can observe. You don't have to talk – you can just be. Being vulnerable and alone opens you up to magical encounters, it also reminds you of how small you are, how big the world is, and how easy it is to disappear.

I've always been drawn to remote lonely landscapes and hidden spaces, derelict, forgotten, restricted, empty – spaces people don't often frequent. Wandering alone allows for spontaneity, you can take risks without putting others' lives in danger. I love exploring hidden stretches of the old Saxon Shore Way, along the Thames estuary, with only wild horses for company and a path that goes on forever. I love seeking solace by a stream, or in a disused artillery fort, a tunnel that few pass through. I would often wonder, whilst out walking, if anyone would find me I were to die unexpectedly. It's a morbid thought, but it sometimes crosses my mind. When I'm lost in the middle of nowhere and it's freezing cold and the sun is going down. Sometimes, I wonder if I could live off the grid. There are so many places I could hide. At times, when I feel especially cut off, I seek comfort in the stories of my brave wandering friends.

I have a lot of brave wandering friends. An older Irish woman named Anne, who recently walked the South Downs Way alone, she also walked the Camino de Santiago. I'd think of Vanessa Woolf, a storyteller and mystic, and Carole Wright, an urban wanderer and community worker. I'd think of my friend Juan, a South American writer who mostly walked and bussed his way to the Amazon rainforest from his home in Colombia. Once he fell asleep in a cloud on a mountain top. He awoke to find the sky had cleared and the day was fast drawing to a close. He was guided down to the base by an ancient Peruvian spirit, a shadow that hurried him towards safety. I love following the journeys and explorations of other wanderers, inspiring real-life people who share a need to escape.

I once took the train up to Chalkwell after a wandering tour. I bought an ice cream and sat by the shore, and watched as the sun sank into the sea. I once watched the sunrise over the Korean East Sea from Dongbaek Island. I used to walk alone through the island almost daily. I'd seek solace under the pines, at the foot of a temple surrounded by flowers on a hilltop. Sometimes while out wandering in lonely spaces, I'd meet another soul seeking solitude.

One morning I found myself settled on the grass by the Jurassic coast beside a deserted derelict path leading down to the clear blue sea below. I was reading an English translation of the Quran. Time passed, a man passed me by. He said hello and I said hello back. On his way back up, we spoke again. We shared our love of space and nature. He was a Dorset Park Ranger. I took out my OS map and asked about certain pathways and he gave me some information.

He asked if I wanted to wander out onto the fields. I said yes, partly out of curiosity and partly because it was nice having someone to talk to. I had been alone for a few days wandering in the Dorset countryside and had spoken but a few words throughout my trip. We drove up in his Countryside Ranger Land Rover to some open land overlooking the sea and settled on the grass. I told him about my enduring dream of being a park ranger. He talked about how lonely it was, and how he could go for days wandering through the empty land owned Ministry of Defense, picking up stray bits of artillery and being silent, mending fences in the freezing cold, the landscapes were sometimes cruel and unforgiving. He said his thoughts would get to him sometimes. We spoke about faith. He said he was a pagan, he worshipped the land, the sun, and the moon. I told him I came to Dorset to seek out peace and spend time with my God. It was nice to talk, to find company in the vastness. After a while, he drove us back to Lulworth Cove and we said goodbye and we never saw each again.

    Wandering alone in the wild is the perfect antidote to the stress and business of guiding in a city like London. After the frenetic summer season, I always seek to escape in autumn. Some years ago, I spent a few weeks volunteering at a youth hostel in Norfolk. I'd go for long, renewing walks by the beautiful Norfolk coast. I'd walk and walk and walk. Autumn is my favourite time of the year. Most people are back at work and school, the weather is good and everywhere is quiet. I love walking by the sea. I walked through the wide and wondrous Holkham beach. I'd pay special attention to my shadow, especially in the golden late afternoon light. Sometimes I would recite an old poem I wrote; "Our shadows are giants, our shadows are friends. Sometimes they guide us. Sometimes they follow us. Sometimes they shrink. Sometimes I think, Umbra Sumus (we are shadows)".

Unexpected discoveries bring about a new and heightened sense of joy and excitement whilst exploring. I once found myself wandering in a wild country park on the Essex border, one stormy grey day. I came by a derelict lodge surrounded with wooden boards and a moat of litter. Curious, I climbed over one of the bent boards and wandered inside the shell of a home. It was so sad and desolate, burnt books with pages torn out littered the floor. As I wandered, I filmed for a while, I filmed the corridors and rooms, the walls were covered with peeling paint, a butterfly floated in from a hollowed window. I felt as though I shouldn't have been there, inside that ghostly house. I could hear wind chimes wail in the distance. I wondered who had lived there and what had happened, and for a chilling moment, I wondered if they were watching me. When I went home later that day, I made a little video using the footage from the ruins and the wilderness - the lake, the heath, the dancing long grass, and crows. It was a sad video, set to Johnny Cash's rendition of Wayfaring Stranger, one of my favourite songs.

I've always been curious about urban exploration. I find the idea of discovering hidden places — forgotten, unknown, unspoken of — alluring. We don't meet people by chance in life - every encounter is meaningful in ways we sometimes struggle to fully grasp. I once made a friend, a friend who turned out to be a soul mate. We have so much in common - we were both spiritual, both creative (he was a filmmaker), both shared a love and need for solitude and exploration - we both worked in the same far-out office block during different stretches of time, we both discovered the nearby Horsenden Hill. I lost my phone on the hill. A few years later he lost his microphone on the hill.

We developed a deep connection that spanned a very long time. We taught each other so much, shared our fears and dreams, watched each other from afar, struggle, fail, disappear, reappear. He would often embark on explorations which involved a lot of risks. He would climb up too high structures, and break into derelict spaces. He would sometimes take a few photos and only share them in real life, with the people he knew. He would embark on adventures at midnight on his bike and not return for days. His way of life was so alluring and dangerous. He taught me about the beauty and importance of preserving precious memories and experiences, having things for yourself. I felt a kinship with him. Sometimes we'd embark on adventures together, we'd bring along packed lunches, a flask of tea and go for long walks sharing deep otherworldly conversation as we went. We met serendipitously on the first public wandering tour I ever led, and often I'm reminded of him, every time I find myself in a very remote place alone, when I see something entirely beautiful and out of this world, and I choose not to share it with anyone. Sometimes it's comforting knowing certain people exist in the world – that lives can be preserved, and our faith can be preserved, especially in a society that has a way of picking and picking and picking at our souls till there's nothing left.

Exploring to Learn

"Being creative has kept me sane and given my mind an avenue to temporarily escape the reality I find myself in" — a prisoner at HMP Dartmoor

Exploration often forces us out of our comfort zone. It is a form of learning – difficult and revealing - these learnings stay with us. We learn wherever we go - museums, community centres, cultural spaces, housing estates, heritage sites, places of worship.

Sometimes I find myself wandering in unlikely places. After a hospital appointment, I'll go for a walk down the corridors, look at the art, exchange smiles, sit in a chapel for a bit, pray in the multifaith prayer room or meditate for a few moments in a secret garden.

Once while wandering around the empty grounds of Bethlam Hospital, after a visit to the Museum of the Mind, I found a chapel to sit in. I began talking to a woman there, a caretaker named Sofia. An hour later, she opened the door to the occupational therapy pottery studios and let me have a wander around. The wall outside was covered in characterful clay faces, inside the studios were fragments of stories of lives endured and lived. Later, I settled in the reading room. I flicked through a zine about a dystopic London, put together by an artist and former inpatient. I flicked through a dozen other books – each book related stories of suffering, of struggle, and a ceaseless search. I read through letters written by patients from the distant past, begging to be released and claiming that they had recovered from ailments of the mind. It echoed a desire and desperation felt by many – to grasp onto hope inside a void, to not lose sight of a glimmer of light in an ever-growing black hole. These learnings are the most powerful, they bring about understanding, and empathy and it is empathy that draws us closer to each other and allows us to cultivate the characteristics we most need to survive and heal – patience, forgiveness, and love.

Before I left, I tarried for a while in the occupational therapy garden, among sunflowers and tomatoes. I wrote in my notebook. The outing had triggered memories of times I had visited friends in psychiatric hospital wards. It triggered memories of suicide notes and difficult heart-breaking conversations. Human beings are so resilient, so extraordinary and courageous – often the people I meet and stories I come by are testaments to the depth and longevity of the human spirit. I seek solace and strength in their stories when I'm at my lowest.

I once paid a visit to someone at Wandsworth Prison. It was a surreal and deeply sad experience; even though I was in it, I felt like I was wholly outside of it. I observed in silence. I noticed everything. Perhaps one way of coping, of making a painful and difficult experience bearable is to take yourself out of it – to be a spectator.

As the prisoners entered into the hall, I watched silently as they unfurled; a series of reunions - the sad kind, the kind filled with lingering stares, unspoken words, pain, sorrow - a collective of souls, longing for a tomorrow that may never arrive. The babies went quiet, the lovers kissed, absent fathers played with their little girls, mothers consoled their aging boys. All the while the clock was ticking, tick-tock, tick-tock, tick-tock.

I remember the canteen tucked at the back of the visitors' hall, the big man behind the makeshift counter with mean tattoos and kind eyes. He took orders as his fellow-worker typed numbers into the till. The queue was long. People bought tea and Mars Bars and Pringles, yellow oval crisps were taken out of the drum and placed into a plastic bag. I remember the colour grey - grey stubble, grey sweatpants, grey walls. The sense of uncomfortable kinship among those from the outside – we breathed in the same choking heavy air.

I remember the small details, colourful drawings on a sterile wall, the worn abacus, a pink busted sofa seat, and a children's book, "Dirty Harry" I think it was, a book about a dog who made a mess. I remember the empty dog cages and the searches, they were violating and dehumanizing - no pocket went unturned, no person went unnamed. I remember the notices on the walls about suicide and chemical substances. I remember the odd things people said, like 'I wish I could have taken my phone in, I would have taken a hundred selfies in prison with my baby and they would have got so many likes', and 'this is his second time inside, the first time was when I was pregnant, ten months after he was back in, he never learned.'

I remember going from one waiting room to another. I remember hearing a familiar song on the radio, it was by Johnny Cash, I Walk the Line, the line, that blurred line. As we left, I remember the tangled barbed wire and the invisible man, from above he shrieked freedom! I want to be free! I remember it all.

Many years later I paid a visit to Wandsworth Prison Museum. It was a small shack at the far end of the prison by the edge of the car park that housed over four hundred items of interest, letters, photographs, maps, handcuffs, and hanging ropes and stories of famous inmates. It was a dark place, but I wanted to learn more. A year later, I paid a visit to the Koestler Arts headquarters, the UK's leading prison arts charity, housed in the former governor's house in the gates of HMP (Her Majesty's Prisons) Wormwood Scrubs. It was an overcast afternoon and I went along with an artist friend. We wandered around the house, it was filled with beautiful, interesting, troubling, diverse art; there were miniature cars made out of matchsticks and otherworldly collages - a clock made of clocks, the hands were all unmoving. Each creation told a story and triggered more memories. Memories I would rarely visit.

I remember getting a ghost bus from Elephant and Castle to a prison out in Suffolk, through biblical pastoral landscapes, under open skies. I listened to a song by J Cole on repeat. I remember reading a moving letter to self in a waiting room when I forgot to bring ID and was refused entry into the visitor's hall. I typed it out when I got home, the letter. It was heartbreaking. It was powerful. I read it occasionally. I bought a book called "Prison: A Survival Guide" by Carl Cattermole. Sometimes, I read "Inside Time", the national newspaper for prisoners and detainees.

I was once involved in a project called 'A Mile in My Shoes' devised by the Empathy Museum. The idea behind the project was simple; walk a mile in someone else's shoes. A pop-up cabin was set up beside the river Thames in Vauxhall. You could walk in and pick out a pair of shoes from a crowded shoe rack. You would then be given a pair of headphones and an audio guide that contained a recording specific to the shoes chosen. You would put them both on, and listen to someone's story while you walked a mile along the river in their shoes. As part of the project, I went on a walk in my local area with a journalist named Emily Elias. She recorded our conversations. I shared memories and stories triggered by our surroundings. In a follow-up email, I shared my shoe size and the brand of shoes I wore at the time - size 6, Vans. On the day of the launch, there they were on the rack. It was a thoughtful and innovative project which enabled you to learn about others in a very personal and moving way.

I've always had within me a deep desire to learn about the human condition and to learn from the experiences of others – sometimes these learnings make me feel hopeless and sad, but sometimes they move me to act, to speak out – to love more deeply and to be always, grateful.

Exploring to Heal

"At the end of the day, we can endure much more than we think we can." — Frida Kahlo

There are few things I find more healing than walking. I walk when I'm angry, when I'm sad, when I feel hopeless and stuck, when I feel alone. I walk when I'm happy, when I'm seeking inspiration. I walk anywhere and nowhere. I walk in circles and a straight line.

There is a healing that comes with exploration, in observing, in seeking out beauty, and finding it in unexpected places. One of my favourite places to wander is Tooting Common, a wild green space not far from where I live. I especially love wandering around the common at dawn, waiting for the sun to rise. It's so quietening and spiritually renewing - to witness the rising fog, the spider's web shrouded in morning dew, to watch a pair of white swans moving together around the lake. There is so much healing in exploring, particularly in nature. Nature heals, it brings us back to our essential self. Nature can keep us sane and grounded, when our outer lives are filled with tumult, to be able to commune with the wilderness and to seek consolation in the bird's sweet song is a blessing. I've walked through Tooting Common countless times in my life. Whenever my heart aches, I sit by the lake and let its waters heal.

I was once sat on a bench by the lake, when a friend — an artist, beekeeper, and community activist — cycled up to me. "I thought you looked familiar!" she said. We caught up for a bit. "Let me show you something!" she exclaimed as our conversation neared its end. She took me to see the remains of a fossilized tree from Dorset hidden among overgrowth, it had been found among dinosaur bones, trilobites, and ammonites. She told that when she was young and tried to picture God, it came to mind - that everlasting prehistoric tree that somehow ended up by the lake. She said she was relieved to see me, to see someone else be with nature, quiet and alone. We went our separate ways.

Time is a privilege, possibly the greatest privilege I've been afforded in my life - time to wander and observe and not just to survive. The older I get, the more I appreciate time, and the more protective I become of it. I love wandering in all weathers and at all times of the day, in places so different. I've walked through the streets of cities and the wilds - I've walked in Fukuoka, Hanoi, Naples, Busan, Paris, Copenhagen. I've walked in Marrakech and Damascus and Cairo, in Sydney and Penang. In my favourite cities on earth; in Lahore and London. Almost every walk has healed something within. It's made me more aware of the world and people. Walking connects us to the seasons, to essential truths - transience and change. Often walking renders us a stranger, it renders us free but often, alone. My experiences of loneliness have continually reminded me of the value of company - and the importance of connection.

In London, wherever I could, I would try to give time to individuals who were seeking company. I'd use CouchSurfing in between meetings or workshops or tours. I would have lunch with a stranger or go for a walk with them. I've met so many interesting people in this way and shared so many interesting conservations - an Italian chef, a Swiss teacher, an Iranian war photographer. Conversations are tools that enable us to learn and grow, they challenge us, our ideas and ways of seeing, conversations are not always easy but they're always worthwhile, especially if your intentions are pure if you're open to listening to other points of view. There is a peace and healing in conversations that connect, that draw you closer to others and to yourself.

As a guide, I often explore with people. My intentions behind being a guide aren't only to show people interesting places and share stories, they're to draw stories out of them, to make them feel listened to, appreciated, and connected. To enable them the opportunity to form friendships and connections with others in the group. It is a form of community building. Guiding is all about exploring, not just places but ideas and philosophies, with the places you visit acting as prompts for others to share their histories and ideas. From gardens, museums, markets - each place is a starting point for a hundred conversations.

The places in and of themselves can be difficult to engage with sometimes. I've come to know London so intimately over the years. I have so many memories associated with so many spaces. There have been times when the city feels entirely haunted - I encounter the ghosts of people who've long disappeared from my life; the echoes of a conversation in a deserted conservatory, in a busy museum, in an empty darkened church. It's a bittersweet feeling, remembering too often, friendships that withered away into nothingness, relationships that faded away too soon – memories connect us. Memories of the places we go and the people we meet, they become a part of us, they embed themselves into every fiber of our being.

I remember talking to Dippy (the dinosaur) whilst on the verge of a breakdown one evening at the Natural History Museum after my shift. I remember wandering around the glass galleries at the Victoria and Albert Museum on my break obsessing over a lost love. I remember watching the birds over the main lake from the observatory at the London Wetland Centre - wondering why I ever returned. We form troubling relations with places, as much as we do with people. But it's these connections, often so complicated, that render places ever meaningful and they come up again and again, in different contexts. On my walks, I encourage people to seek out and reflect on their relationship with places, the possibilities they could possess, and the importance they could come to have in your life. They are the backdrops to our stories. Returning to them, making peace with ourselves – it is often a necessary part of the healing process.

On Play

"Satisfaction of one's curiosity is one of the greatest sources of happiness in life." — Linus Pauling

This morning I watched my little cousin Dulha make a kite using a plastic bag and some needles of wood, he tied them together using a piece of string and let it go. It danced in the sky. He handed me the string after a bit. It was so fun to fly a kite. It soared. With it, I felt myself soar too. I felt a lightness and a freeness.

Lahore taught me the value of play. It was the first time I was around children, children that loved to play games, to run, and fight and laugh. When I was seventeen and returned to London after a brief trip, I decided to spend the summer holidays volunteering as a playworker in a school in Brixton. I loved it, I loved the children and playwork felt worthy, it felt joyous. I spent the days fixing up snacks and playing games like hopscotch and catch. The scheme was aimed mostly towards parents and families who were unable to be with their children during the holidays.

When I returned to Lahore eight years ago, I spent so much time playing. Our house became an almost half-way house for all my wild younger cousins. We'd spend the days exploring, and we'd spend nights eating ice cream and watching movies. I bought them things they wanted, a pet fish, a glue gun. Our conversations would always be more interesting than the ones I shared with the adults, who were mostly just concerned with property, family feuds, and seeing me married. The conversations I had with my younger cousins were inspiring. I loved hearing about their dreams, their dreams of becoming someone, an engineer or singer, of seeing the world. I encouraged their ideas, as zany as they seemed, emphasizing the possibilities of them coming true. I have always struggled with a Peter Pan syndrome, an inability to grow up and to take myself or life seriously in ways that I'm expected to. It was during my time in Lahore I was introduced to someone who worked for a nonprofit called The Citizens Foundation (TCF). TCF provides education for those people who cannot afford it, the foundation operates a network of over fifteen hundred schools many of which are located in villages. I was taken to visit two TCF run schools in two villages. They were beautiful. I visited the classes and met some of the children. I left feeling inspired and determined, to make some kind of difference.

      I realised how privileged I was to have the childhood I had, to have a dad who took us on adventures, to places of magic and wonder. I realised just how much my parents did for me, how very selfless and patient and kind they were. In Lahore, my younger cousins would often complain about being beaten by teachers at school and having afterwards to go to tuition and academy and madrassa, leaving so little time for play – and to be. They were constantly in a state of anxiety, always studying for the next exam, the next paper, the next presentation. Their lives were heavy, busy, and intense, and often on top of that, they were dealing with difficult family issues – issues that caused otherwise kind and loving grown-ups to be impatient and short. I wanted our house to be a place where they could relax and feel free. Freedom was something every child sought. I felt helpless and ashamed of my privilege. I felt that I could have been in their position. My mum enrolled me in a school in Lahore when I was nine years old. We received a syllabus, mum purchased my schoolbooks, a big stack of them. And then we left. I went back to my idyllic primary school Broadwater, enjoyed playtimes and stories and swimming and painting.

      I decided naively that I wanted to run a play-center. I spent a lot of money on toys and arts and crafts activities and decided that was my calling – to provide children the space and means to play. I wanted it to be a safe place for all children, especially poorer children who were struggling to make ends meet - those who picked litter and shined shoes. Every time I came by a child on the streets struggling, my heart broke. I remember on one occasion I met four lovely little boys by the banks of river Ravi, they looked like little men, wearing rags encrusted with dirt and giant smiles. I gave them some money and fruit and told them I'd come back and do something for them. I made them a promise. It's a promise I often think about. My play-centre never opened. I was foolish to think I could make it work at the time. I was young and inexperienced. I vowed to return one day and to make the play-centre a reality. I spent the next eight years in London, working job after job, building skills, and engaging in meaningful community projects.

These days I don't have the same energy, I think I've grown up in some ways and grown wearier in others. I still play catch-me-if-you-can but I don't run as fast as I used to. I still play hide-and-seek and badminton, and ludo, rock paper scissors, and catch. Being around children enables you to see things - the ants carrying heaving loads across the dry concrete, the shapes the clouds make – they help you to truly see and to feel a sense of wonder. So much of my learning is owing to the children I've met and played with. Children enable us to make fools of ourselves, to be curious, to notice things. My cousin Dulha spends ages staring out onto the gully, watching cricket matches and people have a tiff, he notices things. Children give us permission to run and play and create and laugh, and to laugh unapologetically, – to truly feel a sense of joy. Every child is unique and amazing – their power lies in their propensity to forgive, to forget, and to love.

It's hard to be a child in today's world, harder still to hold on to our childlike qualities. Often, being childlike causes others to resent you – and causes you to be more guarded, to be more stoic, and to reveal less of that side of your character. I'm often reprimanded for my ways by those who have a dozen responsibilities – parenthood, for one. I find parents, others, not mine, to be especially critical and unkind. On one occasion, while I was in Sydney, I convinced my brother, and the mother of his children to let my nephews take the day off school so I could spend time with them. They reluctantly agreed. We took the train to the city centre and then the ferry to Manly. We hung out by the beach, enjoyed fish and chips and ice cream and sweets. We went to the botanic gardens overlooking the harbor afterwards. I watched them play fight as the sunset. It was a lovely day - carefree and breezy. The aftereffect of the day was not so enjoyable – their mother and stepmother weren't impressed. I wondered why it was such a big deal, to take off a day of school to create memories that will stay with you forever. Again, I felt privileged for my own experiences in youth – for taking off a day of school and going to the zoo with a friend, or to the pet shop in the market. When my nephews came to London, we spent a lot of time exploring. I took them to the hall of mirrors, to a graffiti tunnel, and to nowhere playgrounds.

    I don't think motherhood is for me, maybe I'm too reckless and free, too much of a wandering bird. Maybe I would never be able to instill within my children a sense of discipline, certainty, and conformity – these qualities have always felt too elusive to me.

    I've learnt to embed play and a sense of lightness in everything I do. I've learnt to see exploring and creating, as a form of play. Playing is writing ridiculous poems rooted in the absurd every day. It's mudlarking by the Thames foreshore at sunrise and counting the planes at London City Airport. It's spending the afternoon in an artist friend's studio with clay and colourful cut-outs, it's molding and sticking. It's singing embarrassing pop songs on a country hike, it's looking out for odd cherubs on the rooftops along Havelock Walk. It's going through racks and racks of fantastical dreamy costumes and masks at the National Theatres' Costume Store housed in a massive warehouse in Oval. It's wondering if you should try on the armory, a Victorian dress, medieval robes, a bloodstained shirt, or an Indian sari – each outfit representing a thousand made-up lives and stories. Play is the joy of exploring the recesses of your own weird imagination. It's wandering around the props store, getting lost amidst giant stuffed animals, rows and rows of suitcases, radios, and telephones, a line of buckets, a black coffin. There's something so special about doing things simply for the sake of joy and to satisfy your curiosity.

    I love climbing trees and was so inspired to read a book called the Tree Climbers Guide by Jack Cooke. One story really struck me – the author, Jack, climbed a tree only to find an older man already settled inside of it, he was dressed smartly and enjoying his sandwich. There's something magical about losing our inhibitions and returning to the things we loved as children. I loved climbing – climbing onto ledges of rooftops and trees. I've always loved to climb trees and to watch from above - feeling invisible and high. I once climbed onto the top of the golden Soviet tank that somehow ended up on some scrubland in Bermondsey. I pretended to be a crazed communist leader. I never wanted to come down. I once wandered around Stockwell Hall of Fame, admiring the colourful, playful, sometimes dark, murals.

    I love skateboarding, I love cycling and I love riding my scooter. I've gone through phases throughout my life, where I've gone back to doing these things I love. Often, I've been made to feel stupid and small for it, but you learn not to care what people think. When I was in college, I'd wander around with my foldable scooter in my bag together with a

Gameboy, wool and knitting needles (and occasionally books). I'd wear colourful outfits when I felt anything but colourful inside. I was so depressed during this period of my life. Playing provided a sense of relief, it also rendered me ridiculous. It takes a lot to be yourself in a world that wants you to be everyone else, but the more regularly you choose to do you, the more you permit others to do the same. To live and let live, to show acceptance and kindness, enables others to do the same.

Play is at the heart of Living London, and my journey towards becoming a renegade guide. I love to evoke a sense of playfulness on all my walks. I loved watching the elders looking at the ducks at the wetlands, impersonating them every now again, laughing and joking and acting like children. Whilst working at an Age Activity Centre, I loved watching the elders play – dominoes and scrabble. I loved watching them draw and tell outrageous jokes and ridiculous stories. I used to love organizing reggae tea dances. I loved seeing them revert to their childlike selves - to dance and laugh and blush and grimace. Play elongates their lives and makes them healthier and happier.

My favourite people are often those with wild imaginations, artists and writers and filmmakers and dreamers. Those who aren't so self-conscious, those who have often had to go against the grain, who possess enough grit and self-belief to persevere with their craft and often do what they do out of love and necessity. Creation comes from play – during the times we feel the least inhibited and free, those are times during which we find inspiration, we let go – of judgments (others and our own), of our worries and anxieties. We become present and enjoy and connect with moments with ease. I especially love artists as they are curious, unselfconscious, and love to play, they give us room to be ourselves and for that to be enough. They don't equate our worth with worldly labels, with wealth and achievement.

I've been so inspired by people who create, people like Khadambi Asalache, the civil servant, exiled poet, and craftsman who turned his ordinary house into a wondrous lavishly decorated work of art. Inspired by his travels and love of beauty, he spent his evenings carving out intricate ottoman-esque shapes from pieces of wood to adorn his home. He read and cooked and threw dinner parties. He never allowed people to take photographs of his home, but wanted visitors to appreciate his creations with their eyes and preserve them in their memories.

Houses tell stories. I once visited Stephen Wright in his techni-colour House of Dreams. His house told the story of his life through his art, through the objects and words embedded in its walls. We sat and drank tea and watched a DVD about his life that had just been delivered by the postman. It was filled with stories, most were sad. Afterwards we talked about stuff like city decay, the car boot sale in front of Wimbledon Dog Racing Stadium, the beauty of Dungeness, and outsider art. We talked about living and dying and creating and trying to channel it all into something that means something to you. And will maybe one day come to mean something to someone else too - for some visitors brought with them ashes of loved ones with whom they wanted to share the experience.

He told me it was usually people who were seeking something in their own lives that were drawn to his house and I told him that perhaps I fit that description. I was at a crossroads, I'd given it all up, and now I was unsure of which way to go. He told me to go East. After our conversation ended, I wandered alone around his playful house, in his studio and in the garden around back. There were all sorts of uplifting and sad things written everywhere, things like *'every day I ask myself what I am doing and why* and *'I go my own way' 'when I'm supporting you, who's supporting me?' 'I have no sense of belonging, where is my home'* and *'spiritually I turned my back on London years and years ago'* and *'dear world, I won't be available for the rest of my life, I'm sorry for the inconvenience this might cause,'* and the house spoke to me, as it was a living thing. For it was felt alive. It was filled with colourful objects, tiny figurines, shiny tinsel, records, mosaics, gem and comb studded pillars, and dolls and models that reflected his life and mundane everyday items that morphed into creatures, and it told the story of his life; his house. Maybe the story would change, but the house was complete. After I finished looking around, I went back into the sitting room and said 'thank you for letting me see and experience your House of Dreams' and he said I was more than welcome.

    I once met Carrie Reichardt, a contemporary artist, in her Mosaic House. We had a cup of tea and talked for a long while, about all sorts of things – loss, community, self-expression. We talked about synchronicity and she told me about the letters she wrote to prisoners on death row, on engaging in craftivism and offering a room to someone who was without. Her work, although serious, was also light and filled with humour and beauty. A sense of playfulness came through with every piece she created, which was reflective of her personality.

    Artists are often up for an adventure, they're always wanting to try new things. I once climbed Beckton Alps, a toxic heap pile with an artist friend Sophie. Halfway up, half-hidden in the shadow of the bushes, we came by a lone man with scruffy dreads and red eyes. He was stood smoking pot, he looked right through us. We kept on walking until we came by a gate, there was a hole in it, we ducked into the hole and wandered up to the summit. From the top of the hill, you could see onto the whole city. "Save the NHS" was painted on iron bollards. We sat on the floor and finished our Slush Puppies – it felt like we owned the city. Exploration and play make life more enjoyable.

On Commuting

"We travel, some of us forever, to seek other states, other lives, other souls." — Anaïs Nin

There's nothing quite like letting time slip away from you on an everyday wandering, under the sun, under the moon, under the stars — to count them as you go.

Over the years, I've worked countless jobs in different areas across London. Often, at the end of my working day, I'd be left feeling depleted, overwhelmed, sometimes anxious, and depressed. On those days especially, I would seek solace in a commute and find refuge in the spaces in between. I've always tried to make my journeys from work to home, as varied and interesting, and life-affirming as possible. I would walk off the stress the day held, quieten the voices in my mind. I would make the most of where I was geographically. My wandering commutes gave me something to look forward to at the end of an often-tiring day.

Whilst working in the Natural History Museum and, many years following that, at the Victoria and Albert Museum, I found relief from the endless noise, crowds, and movement of the museums in the spaces that surrounded them. I would seek out peace and quiet in the beautiful Brompton Oratory. Or I would wander around the picturesque mews, sometimes looking into the wide windows to see others living their lives - cooking and eating and watching TV. I would explore on winter evenings. I'd sit in the churchyard behind the oratory, I would write poetry or call a friend - we'd share ridiculous observations and deep conversations. I would wander around Harrods, people-watch and enjoy free samples in the food hall. I'd often wander back to the south of the river. I'd wander through the pretty streets of Chelsea and cross the beautifully lit up

Albert Bridge. I'd wander into the Herb Garden, and Old English Garden. I'd tarry in St Luke's Gardens, by the tropical-looking palms and towering church. I'd sit for a while with the Gold Buddha at the Peace Pagoda. Spring arrived, blossoms adorned streets and the gardens. I'd write a poem about Shalamar Gardens, by the deserted fountains in Battersea Park, or about the friendship between a weeping willow and a black crow, by Battersea Power Station.

I'd enjoy the solitude, and rarely seek out connection. I'd watch countless sunsets and become aware of the passing of seasons and the passing of time. Sometimes, it would cause me to feel panicky. I'd feel like a lost cause wandering my life away. But mostly I felt a sense of magic and wonder and awe and peace. On summer days, I'd tarry a bit longer, I'd wander through the same routes with friends. We'd enjoy a cup of tea or an ice-cream and lie on the grass. I'd read a book till twilight when I could no longer make out the words. When I was working at the London Wetland Centre, I would always walk from the reserve to Putney along a rather remote and wild stretch of the River Thames. Birds flew over my head, rowers would often row by, and nature always healed something within.

I've always encouraged those around me, especially when they're struggling at work, to carve out a bit of time, if they can, for stillness and for the things that bring them joy. I once led a Poetry Wandering tour in collaboration with a talented poet friend, Samra, in aid of charity. It took place after work and many of my friends from the Victoria and Albert Museum came along. At various points along the way, Samra shared her beautiful work. We watched the sunset by the pagoda and I shared the stories and places I'd been discovering whilst wandering from the Museum every evening after work.

Time is the greatest privilege of all. Having time to do the things that make you feel well is a blessing and something I've never taken for granted or become complacent about. I embedded walking into my daily commutes during a period in which my anxiety was at its worst. I would find it so mentally, physically, and emotionally straining to get on a train in rush hour. So I walked or tarried in places until enough time had passed. I appreciated, so much, my post-work explorations – I valued being able to people watch and to wander and to find relief and wisdom in my surroundings. Autumn was always too fleeting, the leaves turned red and brown and gold, it caused you to look inwards and let go of things that no longer served you or others. With winter, came a period of spiritual rest, and reflection. It was a time to be alone and to cultivate resilience. Spring came and went. Springtime is always renewing, blossoms shroud trees, the light is gentle and pure, the earth begins to awaken and so do you. Summer brings about warmth and connection and a busyness that leaves you feeling enlivened.

My memories of almost every job I've had are often centered around the time before and after work, the geography of the area, mental maps of the spaces discovered, streets trodden, connections made. Every area of London is so vastly different, so unique of itself. I remember getting the bus back from New Cross every day. From the window seat on the top deck, I listened to conversations and exchanges, I watched the world, as the bus passed through Camberwell and Peckham and Old Kent Road, sometimes through windows shrouded in condensation on rainy nights – micro cosmos emerged from bokeh lights. I'd watch the elders and the school kids. I'd make a mental note of the places that the bus passed, greasy spoon cafes and Nigerian Churches, small Christian bookshops, and African food shops.

I remember getting buses to Richmond and Twickenham – when the bus reached its final stop, I would get off and wander. You get to discover the character and soul of a place, or sometimes the lack thereof. I often found the places that looked the prettiest, lacked heart, the energy felt dull - or at least it felt that way to me. I remember on one occasion the trains at Twickenham Station weren't running as there was a body on the tracks - someone had committed suicide. It was a winter's night, and there was a lot of confusion. From a bridge overhead, a college student yelled "I can see the head!" I escaped and walked towards a bus stop in Richmond, all the while thinking about the man who had ended his life. A few months later, another announcement was made on a train; a body had been found on the line.

I remember working on Shaftsbury Avenue. Every day throughout summer, I would go for a long urban wandering after work. I'd wander down Denmark Street, looking at pianos and guitars as I went. I'd wander through Chinatown, through Trafalgar Street, and over the bridge to Waterloo. I'd listen to the buskers sing sad songs, and I'd write poetry. I'd walk to St Paul's, sometimes I'd sit on the secret river steps. I walked, come rain or shine. After a long day in the office, it was the only thing that would keep me sane and happy.

I remember when I worked in Hanger Lane in west London, by the motorways and great big blocks. It felt like a nowhere area, there wasn't much I discovered of note, except for a restaurant – split in the middle – half Chinese and the other half Polish. The décor for both halves was very different too – the owner was the same. One morning while at work, my PC broke down and I decided to go for a wander. I walked up to Alperton before following the Grand Union Canal, past a pretty golf course and quirky colourful houseboats. The towpath was deserted. Eventually, I saw a sign for Horsenden Hill. Curious, as ever, I followed it. Ten minutes later, I was on a wild quiet hilltop surrounded by highland cattle, great big mysterious creatures. My colleague phoned me then to tell me my PC had been fixed, I nonchalantly assured her I would return soon. It was lunchtime anyway, the views were too beautiful. I walked for a bit more, amidst wildflowers and trees shrouded in spring blossoms. Since then, I returned to my hilltop hideaway many times; from it, I enjoyed rainbows, downpours, thunderstorms, and sunshine. I enjoyed many beautiful sunsets and later it became a stop on my Secret Alperton Walking Tour - other spots included a wondrous Hindu temple and Indian specialist shops.

I've discovered many of the places featured in my Living London project, on various wandering commutes - special magical places, often which are open till late - places like Brown Hart Gardens and the Tibetan Peace Garden, and the Poetry Library, and the rooftop of One New Change.

I worked for a year as a Communications Officer for an environmental regeneration charity called Groundwork. I worked across four offices in different parts of London: Lower Marsh, Hackney Central, Shepherds Bush, and Angel. My role required me to constantly be out and about, photographing projects, writing stories, filming - generally doing the things I loved - being creative and connecting with communities. My work took me to places far afield, places in areas of London I'd never visit, places like Plumstead and Abbey Wood, Sutton, Hounslow, Canada Water, and all those places in between. I'd always make a point to explore the area I found myself in before or after I completed my work. I rushed to Lesnes Abbey ruins, before going back to the office. I'd wander through the woods filled with bluebells before arriving at the local community centre. I would follow the River Cray on a summer's evening after filming an event nearby. I'd explore Carshalton Ponds and Honeywood Museum before visiting local schools to photograph assemblies on air pollution. I'd wander up the Albion

Channel before photographing a talent show for musical youth at Canada Water Cultural Space. I'd stick around at the end and help the band load up the van with speakers, drumkits and saxophones, before deciding on the most interesting route to take home. I'd always make up the hours, but the time I was granted in these places was invaluable.

Nearby the offices I was mostly based in, I had mapped out my secret hideaways where I developed friendships with the people who made them special. Places like Old Paradise Yard, a former Buddhist temple that had been turned into a creative community with a café. Or the colourful artists' studios in the sky out of which my friend Chris, a mask maker and mentor worked. Or a church café that often played songs by Bruce Springsteen. Or the Millennium Green where I'd share conversations with eccentric elders.

In Angel, I discovered Culpeper Garden where I met Stanley, a gardener. He ended up telling me the story of his life. When he was eight years old, his mum had an epileptic fit while she was walking along the river in the Caribbean countryside. She fell in and died. She was only twenty-eight. He told me people of the village rushed to his school to break the news to him. Two years later, his dad also died, aged eighty-two. Stanley moved to London to live with his aunt and her two daughters. When he grew older he trained to become a chef. After a whole series of setbacks, he finally made it as a chef though, not long after, he started having epileptic fits. They got so bad he had to give up. Nowadays, Stanley spends his time cooking for people at various soup kitchens and community centres, he also volunteers at the garden - ever giving, ever-smiling, ever forbearing. I also discovered Chapel Market and Duncan Terrace Gardens with its Tree of Heaven. In Hackney, I discovered St Augustine's and the Round Chapel. Every area of London is home to places upon places.

There's something almost alchemical about turning a tedious commute into something wonderful - a necessary trudge becomes an adventure, a time for reflection, creation, inspiration, and nothing at all - just an elongated and unexpected journey home. With it, a sense of purposefulness and purposeless seeps into your life and it makes it more beautiful, or at very least, more bearable.

Travel

"Traveling – it leaves you speechless, then turns you into a storyteller." — Ibn Battuta

This afternoon I found myself wandering through the Itwaar Bazaar (or Sunday Bazaar) on a gully beside Shalamar Gardens, with my cousins and my mum. It was unlike any bazaar I had ever been to. It was colourful and frenetic, and it was a place where people traded in live animals and goods. It was a place that you wouldn't find in any guidebook. The bazaar was filled with small stalls surrounded by crowds. Traders sold all sorts of things, rubies, and gems, and heaps of mismatched shoes, old video cameras, and counterfeit DVDs, and tropical birds and sheep. There were a few stalls selling street food. The dusty gully was narrow, motorbikes trudged through, blaring their horns. Everyone pushed and shoved. I felt like I was in a strange technicolour dream. The experience left me feeling enlivened and my imagination reeled for days. I felt a thousand stories and lives intertwine, in that one lane, on that one albeit brief wandering.

I love being among local people and capturing moments, ordinary everyday moments in less than ordinary places. Had I visited the bazaar the last time I was in Lahore, I would have taken a hundred photos. I would have spoken to the market sellers, I would have asked many questions. I feel as though I've grown up since then, I've developed a sensitivity and deep respect towards people and their traditions. I feel as though I've created boundaries that I am unwilling to cross, for others' sake and my own. Often, I wonder if I could start a tour company in Lahore. I wonder where I would take travelers and what I would tell them - what stories I would share. For some reason, I keep coming up blank. I would never dream of taking them to the Itwaar bazaar. It would feel too much like a spectacle – an orientalism personified. Instead, it feels safer and less disingenuous to write about these spaces, to capture them through words.

A few days ago, two of my cousins' daughters came over for the first time. They were both in their late teens/early twenties. We engaged in small talk for a while. One of the girls, Eesha, asked me if I'd visited Packages Mall, a new shopping centre that had opened in recent years. I told her I wasn't interested in shopping malls. She asked me what sort of places I was interested in. I thought about it for a while before I answered. I told her I was interested in places like the gullies and bazaars and mosques and mundies (vegetable markets). She looked a bit amused. I tried to explain a little better, I wasn't interested in poverty tourism, I just enjoyed seeing the places where local people went, not in a voyeuristic way, but in a way that makes me feel present – that offers new ways of seeing. I was more interested in visiting their universities and seeing where they shopped for groceries. I was interested in spending time at my uncle's restaurant or tagging along to my cousin's school fair. Local people allow you to access spaces, to experience and to understand, in ways that are meaningful. As a renegade guide – this is what I have sought to do.

I love travelling, but it's a quiet love, not a loud love. Travel grants us the things we most need - time and space. It allows for introspection, for revelation, for enjoyment – it connects us to ourselves, others and to God. Our senses are heightened, and we possess greater awareness. We're forced to adapt. We become strangers in a strange land. We become anonymous. We become fools. Often, we struggle with simple things, counting bus fare, discovering train times, the etiquette of visiting certain places, and communicating basic things. On my first day in Busan, I visited a grocery store and spent the longest time looking for things, seeking out the familiar, trying to tell the difference between sugar and salt, and wondering which bread would taste the most like the bread I was used to. Two months on, I came to know that grocery store like the back of my hand. Supermarkets are wondrous places and so revealing of cultures. By the end of my time in Korea, I was able to communicate simple sentences, I developed a deep love and appreciation of Korean food, I would visit the jjimjilbang and loved going for karaoke with my best friend. Busan felt like home, and I wondered if in another life I might have been born Korean.

Travel humbles us. It reminds us of how big the world is and how many kinds of beautiful lives exist within it. It grants us perspective. I've been privileged enough to travel to lands so different, from Syria to Switzerland, Japan to Egypt. Many of my trips have been unplanned and for a purpose, often to visit loved ones. The intention behind embarking on journeys in itself takes away the expectation of travel. Being able to explore has always been a bonus. I love visiting places like Freetown Christiania, an autonomous neighbourhood/hippie commune in Copenhagen, and Monserrat, a mountaintop monastery in Catalonia. There are endless ways to live. I'm reminded of this every time I venture out and witness life unfurl. I value authenticity more than anything, I love wandering around, meeting local people, discovering hidden gems and community projects. Often, I gravitate towards those with a similar mindset. I love connecting with other guides. Once while I was in Vietnam, I went on a day excursion, many of those in my group were guides in different countries – from France to Japan. We traded stories and business cards.

Travel has become glorified and commoditized in often disingenuous ways. I've never truly understood influencer culture. Sacred spaces have turned into backdrops for perfectly curated selfies, in ways that render them emptier. Travel has for many, become more about ticking off places on a list and showing off than anything else.

Aesthetics are seen to be more important than authenticity. I love watching travel documentaries with people like Michael Palin and Levi Roots and Simon Reeves, people who tell authentic stories, who recognize their privilege but try to make journeys less about themselves and more about others and the places they visit. I love documentaries that show the reality of travel – the difficulties as well as the wonders.

Few people capture their experiences of travel truthfully – the stretches of boredom, the anxiety, the disappointment – the very problematic nature of borders themselves. I've developed a difficult relationship with travel, in particular with borders - they've always felt difficult to traverse. I've been interrogated at airports, escorted onto planes and experienced near-death experiences whilst abroad. I've also been very conscious about sharing photographs from my travels.

Travel is a privilege very few people in the world are afforded, and it's a privilege I'm acutely aware of. I have a lot of friends who are undocumented migrants and refugees, who find themselves trapped in time and space, stuck geographically on an island, and stuck mentally – in a state of constant uncertainty. The colour of our passport (or lack of a passport itself) not only places limits on where we can go but also dictates how we live, who we can love, who we can be with. Undocumented migrants, asylum seekers, and refugees suffer so much pain and anguish. Being without leaves them stateless, never here nor there, cut off from families and those around them who will ever understand the struggles they endured to reach the UK, and the struggles they continue to endure.

I once went on 'A Long Walk to Nowhere.' The walk was part of the Whitstable Biennale and led by an artist named Billie (or Elspeth) who I met at Hazelfest, a local arts festival. She told me it was inspired by the work of the

Gatwick Detainees Welfare Group and their walk for Refugee Tales. The walk would explore displacement, disorientation, and the difficulties of negotiating a complex world in a muddy estuary setting. She invited me along. On the day, I showed up at the meeting place outside Billie's studio in Tankerton at low tide. It was late afternoon, the light was gold, and the water still. A small group of women participated. Billie and Kate (who was also leading the walk) delivered a number of interventions that caused us to stop, search (physically and emotionally) and reflect. It was a strange and sad experience – to feel cut off and silenced whilst trudging through mud amidst a watery unfathomable landscape.

    I worked at a refugee and asylum drop-in support service years ago. Many of those who regularly attended had undertaken unspeakably difficult journeys, marked with loss and lack, yet they displayed a resilience that few would understand. I visited Syria many years before the war, while my sister was studying in Damascus. My siblings and I visited the souks and mosques. We people watched. Everyone we met was honest and kind and warm. To see the way people are dehumanized brings about a greater need to be vocal. Connections create empathy. Human stories inspire, causing us to feel compassion, and we need to feel compassion in order to love and want better for others.

    Prejudice and inequality are often at their height at borders. The experiences close friends have had at borders has also caused me to look inwards - to recognize how broken the system is.

    On New Year's Day 2016, I found myself watching the sunrise over Jirisan Mountain in Korea with Chanmi. We never planned our adventure, we just took off on a whim the night before. We ended up driving for six hours until we made it to the deserted National Park. We found a room to crash in for the night, outside of it there were heaps of snow, a burning fire, and a couple of hounds, above, there were a million stars - it was so mystical and dreamlike, that scene. I remember we woke up early the next morning to watch the sunrise before taking off again, to some new unknown destination. That's how we were, that's how we had always been - spontaneous, fearless, slightly crazy.

A year on we were supposed to be reunited in London. I couldn't wait to see her, my friend who over the years had become a close sister to me - closer still. We shared everything; adventures, stories, memories, laughs - so many laughs. I couldn't wait for us to be together again, to witness the dawn of a new year, a new beginning.

I never got to see Chanmi, because they never allowed her across the border into the UK from France. She called me from a police station on New Year's Eve. She said they didn't believe that she was visiting me. She didn't have many clothes or fixed plans, she did have a return ticket though and details of a hostel she had booked. The plan was we'd spend a few days wandering around London, we'd re-live some of our early adventures and embark on new ones, and then when we got bored of the crowds and the buildings, we would take a trip to the South Coast where we'd spend a few days walking by the coast, and talking about the things that mattered - often absurd and stupid things.

They never let her cross the border - the border (real and made-up) that separates people and keeps them apart. They never let her cross. She said she had been detained for over fifteen hours and asked a stream of never-ending questions by immigration officers. "Are you married?" "No." Cross. "Are you working?" "No, I left my job." Cross. "What do you do for money?" "I run an Airbnb." Cross. "What's you're fixed address?" "I currently live on a boat." Cross. "Why do you have so few clothes?" "I don't need very many clothes, I can borrow my friends'." *Suspicious look,* cross. They never let her cross the border. They went through all her things. They laughed at her. They told her she was a suspicious character. They made her cry, they said her tears were crocodile tears. She felt powerless and frustrated and so sad. I could hear it in her voice. I felt her pain.

In this world it's hard to live an unconventional life and not be demonised for it - it's hard to live an alternative life where you don't plan, where you don't have a fixed address, where you don't have a partner or a 'purpose,' you're not driven by materialism, and your sense of self is not reliant on the work that you do or the title that you hold. The things I love most about Chanmi are her bravery, her sense of humour, and the way she lives, freely, unconventionally, unbound by society and people and their small-mindedness. I love that she never asks me how work is going, or what projects I'm involved in - all these too-small questions in a too-big world. Society doesn't like people who they can't put in a box, they don't understand vagrants, wanderers, dreamers - most importantly those with no titles and no need for them; the free. There is a price that you pay for freedom. There is a price you pay for living an unconventional life.

They never let her cross the border. She couldn't believe it, she said she couldn't imagine a worse way to end the year. She told me she would never try to visit Britain again. She said there are far better countries out there, and she'd lived in many of them. She said she only came to see me. Of course, I knew all this. I knew it. All I could do was try to comfort her, tell her everything would be fine- that I'd come out to see her in Paris as soon as I could and sorry she had to go through this. I thought back to when I rocked up in Seoul with a half-packed suitcase, a bit of money, an address scribbled on some paper, and no plans. They let me through. They didn't ask me any questions. It was the first time I had not been questioned at border control. It felt amazing. I felt sad that she didn't experience the same kindness and hospitality I had. I felt sad that I couldn't give her the presents I wrapped the night before, that I couldn't buy her a dozen lunches, and take her on a few hundred wanders. I felt so sad, all I could do was comfort her.

At the end of the conversation, she laughed it all off good-heartedly as she always would. She said they were just doing their jobs, and maybe she was in the wrong. I assured her she wasn't. I told her no one should be made to feel like that, made to feel less than human - I knew how painful it was to be in that situation, to be asked a thousand questions, to be doubted and never believed, to have all your belongings searched, to be laughed at for your inability to live life conventionally – your inability to have lots of clothes, to have lots of money, to have an itinerary, a plan, a plan, a plan. I know what it's like, and it's not nice. There's a price you pay for living free - if you're of colour that is. Maybe only if you're of colour.

Some people come into your life and change it forever. Chanmi is one of those people. She's one of the few people in the world who I can be myself around, the most authentic version of myself. There's something about being around people who are unashamedly themselves, who live day by day and carve out new paths. There's something about people who don't care about fitting in and living a standard life. The system is broken. It has been forever. Chanmi's experience reminded me of this.

Following our reunion in Paris, Chanmi spent three months travelling around Italy alone. Italy was her favourite place in the world, and she had lived there in previous years. Sometimes, it's easy to forget how big the world is, and how adaptable we are as human beings. I've always dreamed of moving to Lahore permanently, but the thought has always filled me with anxiety. Will I feel stuck? Will I be able to adjust – to the weather, the food, the culture? Will I understand others? Will others understand me? Deep down, I know I have the propensity to make it work, but I also know it will be immensely difficult given my upbringing and lifestyle.

We evolve, the things through which we find purpose and meaning evolve too. Since arriving in Lahore, I've spent a lot of time on the rooftop or in my room; reading, writing, watching the world go by. I don't feel that ever familiar sense of restlessness and a desire to be constantly in motion. Sometimes, outward travel can act as a catalyst for inner change. When we're still and away from our familiar surroundings, emotions hit harder, epiphanies are more frequent, and possibilities come into existence. More and more, I can see myself living out a different life here, engaging in community work, maintaining close relations with family, having my own space, and being able to exist without constantly trying to make enough money to live well. Instead, to focus time on giving back.

On Unexpected Connections

"What you seek is seeking you" – Rumi

Synchronicity – magical unexpected encounters, wondrous signs, and unlikely connections have marked my journey towards becoming a guide and have kept me wandering over the years. I love the mystery and sense of possibility that encompasses much of my work, the fact that I never know what I'll unearth, who I'll meet, and what role we will come to play in each other's lives.

I remember the first stranger I met in London, who I came to know as a friend. I was sixteen years old. She stood behind me in a queue at the Imperial War Museum and we struck up a conversation the way people do sometimes. Her name was Jessica; she was a tough seventeen-year-old Latino tomboy who lived in Brooklyn. She was just as bored as me. Maybe that's why we gravitated towards each other. We wandered around the museum talking lightly. She told me she had another month before she had to head back to New York. She wanted to see London and I had time to spare. It felt like the perfect arrangement.

That day we walked from Lambeth North to East London, talking as we went – joking, laughing, enjoying the freshness of each other's company. We walked along the river and through Tower Bridge passing colourful markets and shops. We ate burgers on the stoop of a dilapidated building. She told me all about high school life in the US, about summer school, and her perceptions surrounding British people. I told her about school life in south London, and about growing up in the city. We walked to her Kennington apartment where she was living with her preoccupied brother and his girlfriend, outside we exchanged phone numbers.

The next day I went to see Jessica. We walked again, for hours and hours, we weaved through the markets of Elephant and Castle and passed by the museum where we first met. She told me about her soldier boyfriend and her ambition to join the marines. We walked across London Bridge to the other side of the river, where we looked up at the towering monument. We walked past Mansion House, and Cannon Street and hung out by Saint Paul's cathedral. Jessica was awestruck by it. Neither of us could afford to go inside. We crossed the Millennium Bridge, talking lightly about anything, about everything, her tattoos, NYC gangs, New Yorkers - of needing to know what to do, how to act, and how to get by. We wandered through Borough Market, before getting the tube back.

I met up with her again a few weeks later; we didn't walk for very long that day - just to Elephant and Castle. We bought a bottle of detergent from the supermarket. We said goodbye outside the estate where she was staying and we wished each other luck. Jessica said she'd call me one day, one random day.

In later years I came up with a name to describe the individuals with whom I shared these sorts of brief transient connections. I called them flitters – people who flit in and out of your life, in some ways they're my favourite people, often they're difficult to track down and live lives that are unconventional and scattered.

Almost every walk I've embarked on and every space I've traversed has led to an uncanny connection or a series of them. I once met a man named Howl, by chance, on a balcony of citizenM hotel overlooking the Tower of London. He had it tattooed onto the back of his shaved head, the Tower of London, crows and all. He worked in social care, lived on Cable Street, and enjoyed sunset views from hotel rooftops. He called himself a champagne socialist in jest. I once met a man named Valentine, in Meanwhile

Gardens beside Trellick Tower. He worked as a caretaker at a music label in the 70s and 80s. He once told the Spice Girls off for loitering on the stairs. He told me that back then, they would have bonfires in the gardens, they'd drink and smoke and listen to music and talk all night. I met a white Rasta lady named Sioux and her dog Buxter in the Moroccan Garden. She told me her son was a photographer too and a hip-hop artist and that we should collaborate. I gave her my number - a few days later she called me and told me to come along to a protest demanding cannabis be legalized. I met a smartly suited lighthouse keeper, who introduced me to an inventor. I met a buyer and seller of silver in an underground silver vault. Her name was Linda and she was from Yorkshire. She told me she loved the silver galleries at the Victoria and Albert Museum. I told her I worked there, and the silver gallery was one of my favourite galleries.

Once whilst visiting Ramadan Mosque, formerly a Synagogue, I got talking to the manager, Erkin, or "Egg" as he liked to be called. His dad, a Turkish Cypriot businessman, bought the building in 1977. Egg was now in charge of looking after it. A Hackney boy born and raised, three times Egg tried to run away from the mosque and his responsibilities, and three times he returned. Married to a Jewish woman, Egg has kept a lot of the features of the Synagogue. He is also an undertaker and his time is often taken up by arranging burials. Egg treats everyone as an equal, and helps improve the situation of those around him wherever he can. His best friend told me he had saved his life and the lives of many others. Egg drives a Porsche. He looks after the cats that roam around the grounds of the mosque. His sister runs a café. It became a stop on one of my tours. On a few occasions, his mum would cook members of the tour group delicious Cypriot savouries. Egg ensures that there's a different imam from a different background leading prayer at the mosque every Friday, to keep it inclusive and open. He lends the mosque space to various collectives involved in causes including the Black Lives Matter movement. I told Egg that I would be happy to run a few tours to raise money for the mosque which was sadly in disrepair. It was the least I could do. He told me I was on the right path, and to trust it.

The Living London manifesto sought to draw light onto this sense of interconnectedness. I asked myself, what does it mean to embody a city, to truly live it? What did it mean to me personally, to live London? I discovered it was simply this - a series of unexpected connections. Living London is visiting St Christopher's Chapel at Great Ormond Street Children's Hospital on a late weekday afternoon, it's sitting in silence on a church pew and thinking about all the people who had sat on the same pew before you. It's flicking through a leaflet on its history and finding a photo of a Naomi Blake sculpture at the back. And moments later it's finding yourself outside the small gallery where you met her one night, Naomi Blake, back when you had gone with a mystic who worked at St Ethelburga's, someone you had met by chance at Whitecross Estate and shared an otherworldly conversation with about ammonites and Al Ghazali.

Living London is door knocking at Alverston estate and being invited in for tea by an elderly Venezuelan resident who enjoys growing flowers in his window boxes. It's learning from the gardener who worked there that the railings are made from stretchers used to carry the injured during the second world war and then dropping into the dance studios on your way back to the office only to happen upon a long lost friend in a white room upstairs. It's staring up at the great big cumulus clouds from the bus window in Tottenham, and glancing down only to notice a blue plaque fixed to a wall, dedicated to Luke Howard, the "Namer of Clouds".

Living London is bumping into people you know everywhere you go; street corners, stations, nature reserves, cafes. Living London isn't about making plans, rather it's about following your feet and seeing where they lead you - often you're led to the people and places that are in some intangible way, calling out to you.

Nothing makes me believe more in the idea of the six degrees of separation than being a guide and community worker. I've always been in awe and rendered humble by the way narratives interlink and connections evolve. Nothing ever really happens by chance - every encounter is purposeful and will present you with opportunities to grow, to learn, and to better love others.

I've met many of my closest friends and teachers in the most unlikely places and under unusual circumstances. I met my close friend Lisa at an event I was hosting at a hotel. As part of the event, I was interviewing my sister Sofia who was the founder of a zine and ran a risograph printing press. My younger sister Noreen was talking to attendees when she got chatting to Lisa - the two connected. Lisa was a creative director, she lived in my local area, and had so much in common with my sisters and me. We shared a love for exploring, creativity, and community. Over the years, she taught me to be a kinder and more thoughtful person. We share a deep friendship based on mutual admiration, respect, and love. Through her, I learnt more about friendship, family, and being true to yourself.

I met my best friend Chanmi through a language exchange on Gumtree when I was seventeen. We would explore together, places on the fringes like Epping Forest and Chislehurst Caves. We would disappear from each other's lives for long periods, but then be brought back together again. I never imagined our brief time together in London would evolve into a lasting friendship. A friendship that taught me the meaning of unconditional love and mutual forgiveness. We went from eating fried chicken in South London parks to warming potatoes and mushrooms on a bonfire on empty island beaches on winter nights. Chanmi was a hustler, a sailor - someone fearless and authentic.

I met one of my closest friends at the local swimming pool one winter's evening. A Pakistani girl named Hamna. She was my age, twenty-one, she was funny, fiercely independent, and warm. She struck up a conversation with me in between laps. We clicked instantly. After we finished swimming and got dressed, she offered me a lift home in her beat-up car. I accepted. We listened to Indian music, drove to a café where we had tea, and shared stories of life, love, and everything in between. It was magical. We went on to share hundreds of adventures and embarked on countless road trips. We drove to the countryside, we went on hikes, we laughed together, cried together, dreamed about our imaginary futures, and bemoaned our mistakes and misgivings. Hamna went on to be a dietician, she worked in various hospitals. Often I'd stay with her in towns like Aylesbury and Tring. After work we'd go for long drives, we'd go to eat and explore. One day, her dad met my dad – recognition, familiarity, and joy – they were old friends from Lahore. They came to London together in the sixties.

At a community garden, I briefly met a kind, free-spirited South American poet and environmentalist, Lucia. We developed a strong connection. A few times I stayed with her in Ifley in Oxford where she lived at the time. We would go for long wanderings at twilight by the canal side, we would share our writing and our ideas.

I met another close friend, Spencer, whilst working at a museum. A half conversation marked the beginning of a lasting friendship. She was creative, resilient, and warm, she shared stories of her hometown Niagara where she lived a stone's throw away from the falls. She studied at a castle on the downs. We shared countless adventures - we watched the trains go by from her Walworth rooftop, hiked up Primrose hill at midnight, and wandered down Gallions hill at twilight, singing songs by The Zombies as we went.

There's something so beautiful about discovering the hidden depths of people. The connections I've shared have taught me so much and shaped my way of life in ways that are meaningful and often intangible. The more people I meet, the more I realise how strange and interesting and different all human lives are, and how much we can learn from each other.

I was once approached by a Jewish playwright named Kim. She was a photographer and a traveler; adventurous, and outspoken. At the time, she was living in Berlin. Our lives were immensely different, but for a moment they intersected. We talked for the longest time. A few years on, she was in London for a day and we met up. We went on the cable cars at sunset. We shared stories and insights. We crashed a party afterwards, very briefly, at the Natural History Museum. She was worldly, authentic, and she didn't care what people thought of her. I admired that.

Whilst working at the Natural History Museum, I developed a close friendship with one of my supervisors. He was from Uganda. His life had been varied and interesting. Since childhood, he wanted to be a pastor, but after he lost his faith, he embarked on a journey towards becoming a lawyer instead. We shared long conversations about faith and life and culture. Every day we would ask each other one question – we got to learn about each other in a meaningful way.

I once visited Camley Street, Natural Park, in Kings Cross. I met an older man named Shaun who worked as a Conservation Land Officer. Over the year we became good friends. I volunteered and became involved in practical conservation on the foothills of the North Downs. He would park up his land rover at the corner of Saltoun road in Brixton every week, I'd hop in and he'd drive to the hills.

Alongside other volunteers, I would chop and burn wood to restore the chalk grassland. It was renewing to be outside and to engage in physical work. It made me feel like a human. I'd often tag along to various site visits with Shaun. We shared a love of England's wild spaces, maps, stories, and solitude. We shared a love of literature and art and found that although we came from immensely different backgrounds, we had so much in common. Once we embarked on a long hike in the South Downs – we drank tea and ate samosas on the way. We pointed at spindly trees and the birds overhead. We ended our walk by the sea at twilight.

The internet also allows for the formation of connections. I used to write a blog, a very long time ago. One of my readers, a young Pakistani man – an engineer and a spiritual seeker–became my pen pal. We would write to each other. He bought a book I wrote (which I briefly made available for people to buy), 'This Restless Soul.' It was an accumulation of experiences, stories, and journal entries I had gathered and organised into a narrative over a period of six years of my life. It was mostly about the spiritual struggle. Sometime after he read it, we both became involved in a project which sought to connect people of colour to the National Parks and encourage them to share the parks with others through leading trips and excursions.

On one occasion, we all came together for a weekend to engage in a programme of activities like orienteering, practical conversation work, and kayaking. I met him there, it was beyond surreal. We talked. He mentioned my book on many occasions, I felt exposed but comfortable. I stayed on at the end of the trip and spent another day hiking alone. I thought of him. We wrote each other for a while, long emails about our lives and faith. He lived in Ireland at the time. He posted my books to me with some edits he had made, both 'Freegan Freedom' and 'This Restless Soul'. We were so different, he liked to take calculated risks, he rode a motorbike, and was a lover of mathematics. I was floating. Our unlikely friendship came to an end when he got engaged. Every connection, every encounter is meaningful. He encouraged me to continue writing and instilled within me a belief that I had something to say.

I'm more comfortable than most with the idea of transience. I have faith that people come into our lives and leave them for a reason. I believe that the opportunities to connect and reconnect are endless. Everywhere you go, you're presented with an opportunity to truly understand yourself and another human being.

I would often lead group visits for students from an English language school in Wimbledon. I came to know the Social Programmes Lead. She was a lovely Spanish lady named Blanca. She introduced me to a whole new world. She lived in a beautiful historical home, with her family as well as a Colombian author and a Syrian refugee. I became friends with them both. We shared so much in common. Juan, the author, had a million stories to tell - in his younger years, he had walked from his home in Colombia to the Amazon rainforest. He had bathed in crocodile-infested waters. He had walked in the Andes, guided by spirits. Tamer, the aspiring actor and refugee who had walked to Britain from Syria. He had lived in the Calais Jungle. Both taught me so much.

At a women's business event, I sat next to a woman who later became one of my closest friends and mentors. An older Irish woman named Anne, who was starting up a business at the time that involved creating beginner kits for hikers. She had walked the Camino. She was open-minded and interesting and has so many stories to share.

When I was in school, I had a close friend named Tara. She was wild and interesting. We shared so many adventures, a day out to the farm (she tried to steal a chicken), to the beach (she brought drugs), to a little-known suburb (we ended up watching CCTV footage in a chicken shop). During our last year of school, we quite seriously decided that we would go to college together in Lahore - a place called Beaconhouse. We carried out the research, sorted out visas and admissions, we somehow convinced our parents it was an acceptable idea - and then things fell apart. We never went. After we started college, our paths diverged and we drifted apart.

I randomly bumped into Tara three years later at my university, Goldsmiths, where she told me she was studying psychology. I bumped into her on the day of an art show I had put on with a friend named Emer. It was taking place in a gallery off Vyner Street in East London. I pleaded with her to come — she did. We wandered around all the galleries of Vyner Street that night, arm in arm and it felt like we were never separated. We embarked on a few old school adventures. Predictably, we lost touch again.

The synchronicity that has forever graced my journey, has helped me to feel safe and connected to something so much greater and more beautiful than I can imagine. It has drawn me closer to God and has reminded me constantly of the fragility of life, and the possibilities that each day holds.

Travels can present us with synchronicity too. I remember a friend and I bumped into a young Moroccan man we met on our first day in Marrakech in Jemaa el-Fna - he introduced us to a friend who organised excursions for travelers. On the last day, we met again by chance and the three of us walked around all day, we ate together and we went to Menorah Gardens. It felt real and special. At the ferry port in Busan, Chanmi and I bumped into her boat dealer friend. The world feels much smaller, much kinder, and easier to navigate, the more we experience the magic of unexpected encounters.

Wandering Connections

"Attention is vitality. It connects you with others. It makes you eager. Stay eager." — Susan Sontag

Over the years, I've made countless connections through my wandering tours. I've met people who are interesting and innovative, who share a similar positive outlook, a curiosity, and openness. I used to especially enjoy leading private wandering tours for individuals and small groups.

I love that I never know what to expect and that for the most part, people are so willing to share things. I once led a walk for an older gentleman from Sussex. He worked in community planning and would go sailing in his free time. He told me a story of the time he met Kate Winslet, she approached him on a paddleboard. She looked rather ordinary. I met a black American nurse, who was so positive and kind, who shared her experiences of college life in America. I met a Mexican journalist and a Brazilian housewife. I met two lovely Spanish friends, who attended the same university as me, shared a passion for community projects and a love for London. I met a Saudi Arabian interior designer, an Asian American from San Francisco who ran a woman of colour hiking group. I met talented and bright art students. They ended up making an animation about me and my explorations. I met a film editor and an urban planner and software engineer and doctor and psychiatrist. I met many teachers from Germany.

I met two lovely Swedish friends. They commissioned me to lead another walk for their women's group a year later. They invited me to an event at Brixton in a beautiful workspace, and months later, I was offered a free desk to work at in that very space, it afforded incredible views across the city and I somehow ended up being on the same floor as many founders who inspired me and colleagues I'd worked with over the years. You never lose out by being kind and paying it forward, the universe has your back and will help you find a way to keep going. Sometimes, you just have to have faith, to let go and give your life to God, and trust His plan for you.

Sometimes the connections are quite haphazard. I remember once a lady barged my sister in a coffee shop. She looked a bit like Joanna Lumley. She showed up for my Secret Gardens tour ten minutes later. She was posh and eccentric and my sister and I warmed to her towards the end of it. It turned out she knew a man named David who worked in pantomime and volunteered at the London Wetland Centre while I was working there. I remembered David. He once gave me a hard time for not knowing who Mark Owen was when he came in. I asked him to spell his last name for Gift Aid Donation. "How could you not know who he is, he's only part of the most popular boy band in British history!" He exclaimed condescendingly. He did the same when I rang up Frank Lampard's shopping. Well, I guess it figured. I met another lady on that same tour, halfway through she exclaimed, "I know you! We met at Stefano's Spitalfields tour". I smiled and nodded. Stefano was another renegade guide friend that I had crossed paths with. He and his wife and baby had come along to a Secret Wandle Wandering I once led. One afternoon I was at the Museum of London for a meeting, when a young woman called out to me. "I was on your tour yesterday, the one you led in Brixton for students from Ithaca!" I didn't recognize her at all, but smiled and said "Yes! So nice to see you again!"

Sometimes, unexpected encounters are more ridiculous than anything else. On my Secret Dalston tour, I would regularly pass by a wondrous colourful house. After a bit of digging, I discovered the story behind the house and the story of its owner, Lennie Lee. He was born to Jewish parents in South Africa. He was an artist and a collector of counterculture art. I read about the wild 'fake wedding' parties he threw, back in the '70s when people married for passports. I read about the months he spent in Europe after he graduated, where he would visit museums and galleries by day and sleep rough by night. He bought the house when it was falling apart. Many of the houses on the street, at the time, were occupied by squatters and artists. He married a mime artist. He seemed to have a larger than life personality. I contacted him once, asked if he would like to have a cup of tea and a look at his art.

It became one of the stops on my tour, tourists would take photographs of the colourful house and I'd point at it and share stories surrounding the home, and how homes were reflective of their owners. Sometimes I would see him take the trash out, he'd be wearing his pajamas and he would stop to look at us from across the road. Sometimes, someone beside me would wave and he would look on blankly. For a while, I was worried he might file a restraining order against me. Then one day, a year on from when I sent him an email, he replied. He invited me to his house. I went along, excited to finally meet him. I was determined to find out more about his house and his life. I rang the bell and stood on the pink porch awkwardly. I waited. I rung the bell again. I waited some more. I called his number, but he didn't pick up, so I left him a text message. I posted a bar of dark chocolate and a postcard with some kind words written on the back through his letterbox. The next day, he left a voice message on my phone, together with three WhatsApp messages and a text message. He was deeply apologetic. He said he was in the attic and didn't hear the bell. He asked if I would be able to come by again. I said maybe in the future. I don't know if he was being earnest or not, but I never saw him again.

Being a London guide, especially a renegade guide, makes the world feel a lot smaller and often, a lot more friendly. You meet the same people, again and again, in different places and a different context. It's taken years to get here, and I appreciate every positive (and negative) wandering connection I've made.

A Tooting Wandering

"Freedom for Tooting!" — Wolfie, Citizen Smith

One tour stands out in my mind for being especially memorable - as it unfolded, so too did many fragmented stories. It was a Secret Tooting Tour I would often run in my local area.

I walked towards Tooting Broadway Tube station, the meeting place for the tour. When I arrived, two strangers were already there waiting. I shook their hands and we made small talk for a few moments. The young woman said her name was Bea, she told me she came along to a Wanderers Storytelling Social I'd recently organised. She'd bought the Tooting Wandering Tour tickets for her friend's birthday. Her friend introduced himself – his name was Luke. It turned out he volunteered as a guitar tutor at the Recovery Café (which by day was the Age Activity Centre where I worked and Boy George's former workshop). He knew all the clients and staff, and I remembered hearing many nice things about him. Anne showed up, my friend and one of the speakers at the Wanderers Storytelling Social. She brought along her friend Nadia, a lovely Egyptian lady who I later came to know. Other attendees included a young lady named Poppy, who found out about the tour through an article I had written for Huck magazine on the gentrification of Tooting Market and a couple who had recently moved to the area. Lastly, my brother's partner Juliette arrived.

It was an overcast Sunday morning, but the streets of Tooting were as busy as ever. We wandered into our first stop, Buzz Bingo Hall, housed in the beautiful Grade II listed art deco Granada cinema. I shared stories of the elders from the Age Activity Centre who frequented the bingo hall, and information on the history of the wondrous building, the musicians that played there including The Beatles, Frank

Sinatra, and the Rolling Stones. I took the group upstairs to the hall of mirrors and to the theatre. I told them that I'd sometimes see an elder reading a paper in the dark or sleeping in the auditorium overlooking the stage. The bingo hall was a place for people to go, especially older people who were socially isolated. It felt like a time capsule. I shared stories of other bingo halls, like the Palace Bingo Hall in Elephant and Castle. It was the largest bingo hall in the UK. I talked about the owners, characterful South Londoners, the vintage knowledgeable kind, and the communities that you'd often see. I shared the story of Joy, the lady in a penguin suit who handed me a gold membership card, and with whom I shared a birthday and many laughs, and the woman who exclaimed 'Sister, gambling?!' I shared the stories of the Caribbean elders wearing top hats and baseball caps, smoking cigars on the rooftop balcony. I listened to members of the group as they shared their own stories and I watched as they wandered around and took photographs.

The next stop was Tooting Broadway Market. I shared stories of my childhood, of a time when my aunt worked at a stationary stall in the market and I would keep her company and enjoy free popcorn from the man who ran a popcorn stall opposite. I shared stories of the stallholders, CJ who ran the music shop, and Mr. Singh who sold fabrics. I talked about gentrification and community. I shared stories about other characterful markets across London, East Street Market where the opening sequence to Only Fools and Horses was filmed, and Ridley Road Market where you could purchase produce from all corners of the globe. I talked about the community canteens where I worked, and the story of my friend Paul Yarrow who was voted the 46th most annoying man in Britain on a BBC3 countdown. He was known for photobombing hundreds of live news reports, with his trusty shopping trolley by his side. He was a hero – a soft-spoken, quirky, knowledgeable socialist.

We walked to the car park behind Iceland. The walls were covered with colourful graffiti murals. I often led the walks by night, I would bring a torch along and point it at Popeye the Sailorman and Wonder Woman. I told the group about other graffiti yards, Stockwell Hall of Fame, and the Trellick Tower yard, and the graffiti that stretched the length of Parkland walk. You could walk the disused train line, between two platforms. I told them if they ever embarked on the walk, to look out for the mysterious Spriggan, a legendary creature from Cornish faery lore. I told them of the signs and stories behind some murals. I told them of places like the Banksy tunnel, how on the day I decided to quit my job, I saw the words 'If you're looking for a sign, this is it. Just do it' freshly sprayed onto the wall. It reminded me of the story of my mudlark friend Nicola, who on the day she needed guidance, found a message in the bottle that read something along the lines of 'don't follow the money, follow your heart.'

I told them of the story of leading a walk in Brick Lane, by the Nomadic Community Gardener and meeting a street artist by chance. He told the group about his journey, he told us about Berlin in the '80s and what street art meant to him and people of his generation. As we were about to leave the car park, I told the group that I was sure that someone was living in a tent in the car park at one point. Poppy said it was her friend who lived in the tent. I wanted to know more. I planned to ask her about it at the end of the tour, we had agreed to go for lunch together at a local Dosa cafe.

We walked over to the next stop, Streatham Cemetery, a beautiful wild cemetery home to goldfinches and green woodpeckers. I told the group stories surrounding the cemetery and how one of the chapels was going to be converted to a community centre and how valuable green space was in Tooting. I shared stories of bat walks and elderflower cordial, of the apiary, tucked at the back of the cemetery where my friend Lucy looked after bees. I mentioned some of those who had been buried at the cemetery, obscure figures, like animal impersonators and a vegan pioneer. I told them I'd sometimes wander through the cemetery when I cut class in school. I told them I once worked for a regeneration charity that restored a pathway and reopened the Broadwater Gate of the cemetery. I told them about friends who worked in cemeteries, who told stories of magic and the occult in derelict spaces. I told them about the experiences people had in cemeteries and spaces like the Death Café.

I spoke of the Magnificent Seven cemeteries in London, High Gate, and Abney Park and Nunhead. I shared the story of an older man I met once at Nunhead cemetery, he was a member of the 'Friends of Nunhead Cemetery' group. He had frizzy hair and wore tweed and was fascinated by cemeteries. He and his wife had been around the world in 80 cemeteries, he'd been to cemeteries in Mexico and India. I shared stories of some of the cemeteries I'd visited, in Lahore and Paris and Marrakech. Cemeteries are so revealing about society's relationship with death. I told the group about Golders Green Crematorium, where the ashes of Sigmund Freud and T.S. Eliott remained. I told them of the peace and quiet that enclosed the gardens, they were filled with almond trees and magnolia trees. From the cemetery, I pointed out other green spaces in the area, like Tooting Community Garden, and Tooting Common and Share Community Garden. I told them about meeting Eve, in a garden of Eden, and how she plucked off a ball of too-green lettuce and handed it to me.

I told them about other hidden gems in Tooting – the scrapstore run by Sascha, Oily Cart with its gold lift (the HQ of a children's theatre company that specialized in creating multi-sensory productions aimed at children with disabilities), the lido where a scene from Snatch was filmed and the specialist shops that added character and soul to Tooting, shops like Little India and Daily Fresh. On some Tooting tours, we would carry on walking and I would tell a few more stories. Sometimes we would visit the beautiful and sad grounds of Springfield Hospital and sometimes we would visit the Sewing Machine Museum filled with old singer sewing machines and the private collection of the Rushton family, some members of which I'd come to know.

The tour ended back at the entrance of Tooting Market. We exchanged goodbyes and Poppy and I went to have lunch. We spoke in length about Tooting and what a magical interesting area we lived in. She told me about her friend who lived in the car park behind Iceland. She was a young homeless woman with blue hair that I had seen around. She had come from America and her name was Emma. She was married to a man named Amir. When her mum got cancer, she had to sell her tattoo parlour to pay for her treatment. She and her husband decided to come to London where she had family. Her family was unable to offer them support or a place to live, and so they lived on the streets for years. They were both so young. She told me stories of the loss and abandonment they endured, and how she had tried to help. After a very long and difficult journey, they had both finally found a place to live. Emma had a baby. I remembered a brief interaction I shared with Emma a few years ago. I delivered her a meal from the community canteen where I worked at the time, it was a brief interaction. She smiled, grateful. I told Poppy that she would be blessed for all that she's done.

We said our goodbyes after we had finished our meal and our conversations had come to their natural end. The Tooting Wandering was emblematic of why I had started to guide and the beautiful connections that emerged from my work. Many of my walks over the years, in areas across London, from Hounslow to Hackney, Erith to Ealing, have been filled with interactions that instill within me, gratitude, wisdom, and hope.

Patterns in Our Lives

"Life can only be understood backwards; but it must be lived forwards." — Soren Kierkegaard

When I visited Copenhagen, I made a note to visit the grave of Soren Kierkegaard, the Danish philosopher, poet, and theologian. His words "Life can only be understood backwards; but it must be lived forwards," deeply resonated with me. It was the premise upon which my book This Restless Soul was compiled. I sought to identify the patterns and the recurring themes present in my life - to make sense of time, connection, and growth. My book, which was essentially a very layered and long diary, provided me with direction, hope, and reliance in the unseen. Here in Lahore, I've been rereading parts of This Restless Soul. I've been especially drawn to the parts I wrote on previous visits to Lahore. I've realised that everything that's happened since the last time I was here, has been meaningful. Somehow, we end up travelling a path that was meant for us. I've learnt that often things fall into place and sometimes things fall apart. I had a vision, a myriad of visions for myself, many of which subconsciously manifested.

    I feel a lot of remorse and sadness reading back and trying to remember the person I once was. Sometimes, I feel like that person no longer exists. The decisions we make, our most trying struggles and triumphant successes, they change us. Often, we lose our way and we lose our words, we end up far from where we envisioned ourselves to be. We sacrifice everything for nothing. Sometimes we find ourselves bereft in a nameless future we never wanted, but eventually, we find our way back again.

    Unexpected encounters make life interesting – sometimes it takes one person, one conversation to change everything – to alter the direction we chose to go in and the thoughts and emotions that lead us there. Sometimes it takes one unexpected encounter with one person to trigger an epiphany. Synchronicity often makes me feel like I'm on the right track in life – to ask God for a sign, for a miracle - and to be patient as you wait. I'm learning again to be patient.

On Faith

"Be not entangled in this world of days and nights; Thou hast another time and space as well." — Allama Muhammad Iqbal

This morning I paid my respects to Allama Muhammad Iqbal, a poet I greatly admire, at his tomb beside the beautiful Mughal Baddashai Masjid. Together with my mum and two of my female cousins, Arooj and Mobeen, we wandered through the courtyard of the masjid. A group of grey pigeons circled its beautiful ancient towers and spires. Inside, an old man was reading the Quran and a few women were praying. We settled on the ground after prayers. It was so peaceful; the clouds were heavy and thick and filled with water – soon to scatter down onto the earth.

My favourite mosque in the world is Wazir Khan masjid. It's a masjid I've traversed on many occasions, it's technicolour and magical, hidden in the old city within the folds of old Anarkali. To reach the mosque, you have to walk through an ancient faded lane, home to shabby stray cats. On each side of the lane, you'll find dark rooms side by side. In each room, someone is doing something. The shoemaker is making shoes, the clothmaker is making cotton, the ironsmith is shaping iron. It is ageless and shrouded in mystery. At the end of the lane, as you turn a corner, there stands the masjid. It's so beautiful – in part crumbling - upon every visit, I feel my soul exhale.

There is no greater feeling in the world, to me, than that feeling of closeness to God. Throughout my life, many of my dreams have remained rooted in the ethereal and the spiritual. I've always sought to better my character, to be more selfless and to increase in faith. I've always sought peace over fleeting joy, peace, perfect peace.

I've gone through periods in my life where I've felt like I was so close to where I needed to be and who I needed to be and other times, more often than not, I feel so far away. I dwell in my disasters and go around in circles with certain doubts and trying vicissitudes. Too often I lose faith in myself and my ability to truly grow - to become the person I'd like to be – authentic, loving, truthful and forbearing. I have been at constant war with my lesser self, to be better, to make better decisions, decisions that cause others joy and not pain.

My journey towards becoming a guide has been deeply spiritual. It has forced me to confront the lack within - my weaknesses, my failures, and my dysfunctions and to find peace in God and resolve within. Faith has guided me, grounded me, taught me, reprimanded me, given me courage and hope. Sometimes, something grows out of the nothingness. And God – Allah - has been my ultimate guide. I often find myself reflecting on a certain verse in the Quran, whereby God says to the Prophet Muhammad (peace be upon him) 'Your Lord has not taken leave of you, [O Muhammad], nor has He detested [you]. And the Hereafter is better for you than the first [life]. And your Lord is going to give you, and you will be satisfied. Did He not find you an orphan and give [you] refuge? And He found you lost and guided [you], And He found you poor and made [you] self-sufficient.'

I take comfort in knowing that my Lord is with me. I feel His presence, it's more pronounced during times I find myself lost and found. I take comfort in knowing that this life is almost a prelude to another life, a more lasting and real life. As a guide, I'm so inspired by the stories of spiritual guides, and spiritual seekers, both from the past and in the modern world we live in. I am constantly inspired by them – their propensity to give, to love, to be patient, and to move others. I pray always, that the guidance that I give and the guidance I receive is rooted in love and truth.

The Stranger's Journey

"Be in this world as though you were a stranger or a wayfarer." — Prophet Muhammad (Peace be Upon Him), Sahih Al-Bukhari

I've always been drawn to worlds beyond the one we reside in. I've always been drawn to the spiritual, the intangible, the unseen – the mysteries that surround us. When I was a child, I developed a love for prayer. I loved talking to God. I loved hearing stories about prophets, and spiritual seekers. I loved learning about miracles. I often prayed to God to grant me a magical and interesting life. Like my father, who came to London and lived a rich life; like my brothers who travelled, and often lived nomad lives in far-flung places. I remember at school in Year 6, we were made to create a project book on someone who inspired us. I chose to do mine on the Prophet Mohammad (peace be upon him). I learnt so much about his life, his character, his teachers – the struggles he faced and the difficulties he overcame. I was twelve years old at the time. It was the first Ramadan during which I kept all my fasts. At break times, I prayed in the classroom. I decided (for a brief while) that I wanted to wear a headscarf. In ways, I think I reached my spiritual peak when I was a child. I felt so connected and so clear on what I felt my purpose was and who I wanted to be.

    I drifted only to begin again down a spiritual path in my late teens and early twenties. I read the Quran and scriptures like Imitation of Christ and the Journey of Strangers. I read about the lives of Sufi's like Al Ghazali. I was inspired by the stories of the prophets, and almost envious of the deep connection they shared with God. I sought lessons in the stories of Moses and Noah and Jonas and Joseph. The story of Joseph moved me the most. I felt humbled and in awe of prophets that found themselves in the darkest of places, at the bottom of a well or in the belly of a whale , and yet held onto hope and continued to believe. I greatly sought the qualities they possessed – the propensity to endure, to forgive, to love. I sought comfort in the stories of strangers. To live as a stranger or a traveller, is to be in a state of (often) vulnerability, reliance, and openness. Strangers have no roots, they aren't anchored to people or places in concrete ways, rather they forever seek a lasting closeness to God. I've always sought to be a stranger and to live like a stranger – these stories and the idea that a stranger is someone worthy of blessings have always comforted me and helped me to resolve myself with an almost permanent sense of detachment I've felt towards others. Rather than being reprimanded for being in this state, I feel like spiritual teachers celebrate it. Blessed be the stranger. The one who seeks neither glory nor praise, he goes unnoticed and unblamed. I often think about Khidr, the mysterious spiritual guide who crossed paths with those who sought to find God. I think about the way he guided Moses who once accompanied him on a journey. He guided him in mysterious and perplexing ways.

    I've always admired those who turned their backs on the world in order to live a monastic life, a life of service. I've often wondered if there was a vocation, like that of the Christian nun, in Islam. When I was nineteen, I embarked on a pilgrimage that tested my faith. I became very sick and almost died. I felt like I had been abandoned by God, as though I was not worth saving. My soul and body felt as though they were escaping me. I remember on the coach to Mecca from Medina, I looked up at the stars in the sky above the mountains the entire journey and begged to be healed. When I finally reached the Kaaba, I felt a sense of inexplicable joy and euphoria. Together with my sisters at either side, I circled the Kaaba. We completed the pilgrimage and I became very sick again. I prayed. I promised God that if He spared me I would dedicate my life to helping others. One night before we left Mecca, I met a guiding angel in the form of a little girl from Sierra Leonne. She had one arm; her other arm had been severed in a bomb attack. She held my hand and followed me around for part of a night. I gave her what I could, and we parted ways. I felt very small and insignificant, but more than that I felt very grateful and even more determined to keep going down the path I had begun down – to have patience and to persevere.

Before I left for pilgrimage with my family, I felt I had reached a peak in sincerity and pureness of faith. I'd embarked on a journey that led me to experience a spiritual clarity, a certain euphoria, and a closeness with God that I have never felt since. Sometimes I wonder what would have happened if I had departed from the world whilst on a pilgrimage and whether it would have been a blessed death. For since then, I've died a hundred spiritual deaths. I've made so many mistakes and experienced so many failures. I wonder often if I would have had a better chance of salvation if I had died then and there. This is a difficult thing to explain to those who haven't been on a similar journey.

During the last decade, I have experienced so many highs and lows when it's come to faith. I have spent years and years at war with myself, trying so hard to be consistent, to practice what I know to be true and to not give up on the path, especially during times I feel empty, abandoned, hurt, and hopeless. So many times, I have found myself in desperate need of healing; physical, and spiritual. Often during these times, I seek solace in solitude, in walking in lonely spaces for days and days, and talking to God.

One autumn I took a few weeks out to volunteer in a youth hostel by the coast. Every morning I'd wake up at 5 am and start my chores at 6 am. I'd serve breakfast to those staying at the hostel; school groups, lone elders, wayfarers, and runaways. I'd then spend the next few hours scrubbing toilets and changing beds. I felt like I was living a monastic life. Once I had completed my shift, I'd walk for hours and hours by the sea. The salty windy sea air was thoroughly cleansing. I'd walk barefoot on the sandy shore, the cold waters would crash against my legs and the sun would warm my bones. I slept well. I felt well. I felt free. I didn't have my phone or my laptop. Sometimes I'd go to the small library, the only one in town and I'd read books on nature and solitude. Most of the people who lived in the town were older white pensioners. They were friendly, sometimes curious. On a few occasions, I felt like an alien, but mostly I felt a sense of joy.

On another occasion, I went to Liverpool and spent a few days wandering around. I hiked down to the pine woods and across the golden sands of Formby Beach. I travelled to the Lake District in Cumbria. I stayed in a hostel, by night I'd sit in the canteen and drink tea and write and talk to other wanderers. I've found that solitude often transitions into a deep loneliness when I no longer feel the presence of God when I'm alone. A creeping darkness overcomes me, a sense of dislocation. I've learnt to move through these stretches of time - however isolating and pronounced they are. I find the sea calms me and brings me a sense of possibility in my darkest periods. When I was in Melbourne and Busan I would often seek refuge from my thoughts and worries by embarking on long walks by the sea. I've always dreamed of living by the sea. I always feel more connected to God by the sea and at dawn.

I've embarked on many dawn walks in London, in places like urban Walworth and Camden to the green wild spaces of Wandsworth. While the world is deep in slumber, I recite prayers. I wander. I seek out the signs of God in the spider's web covered in morning dew, in the spring blossoms emerging from the fog, in the singing birds and the rising sun.

Everything we go through makes us everything we are. It makes us stronger, more compassionate, more loving. The jobs I've taken and the work I've done, all reflect my faith and my desire to live it, to be the best I can be, to be kind, mostly to be kind. I care less about what people think and more about what my God would think. In a world that is in many ways rooted in the unreal, my faith grounds me. It opens me, my mind and my heart, and it is a source of endless joy. I ask for miracles and I ask to be guided. I ask that my tours go well and that they are a brief source of inspiration, connection, and happiness.

Somehow, I always felt like being a renegade guide was a vocation befitting of a stranger – to wander, to be lost and found, to accompany others, to be entrusted by them, to share truths and stories that inspire – stories of modern-day mystics, and community leaders and spiritual teachers and everyday people who are rendered extraordinary owing to the acts of kindness and courage they put forward. You grow through learning about, and often emulating, others, their qualities, each unique to a person – generosity, humour, positivity.

Spaces and Faith

"The heart is the hub of all sacred places. Go there and roam." — Bhagawan Nityananda

As a guide, I've explored many different faiths through the places I go and the people I meet. I've met nuns from Belarus at a Russian Orthodox Church who relayed to me stories of service and saints. I've wandered through temples and listened to elderly Indian women chant prayers in unison. I've sought shelter from heavy rain in the grounds of a Buddhist Temple, outside the house of a monk. I've sought quiet in countless churches across the city, in oratories, and cathedrals. I've prayed in mosques and watched others pray in synagogues. I've conversed with pastors and priests and gurus and the faithful.

    When everywhere else is closed, I find a place of worship to seek solace in. Once while I was in Sydney, I found myself in a difficult position. I had nowhere to go and so, as dawn broke, a friend and guardian angel, dropped me off outside a mosque in Auburn, a multicultural suburb. I prayed most of the day there. I left for a while to have lunch and then returned. After the last prayers, the mosque was closing. I wondered if I should hide out in the toilets and sleep there the night. I didn't. Instead, I wandered the streets of Auburn till midnight.

    When I was sixteen, my little sister and I took a trip to Stonehenge. Our train stopped in Salisbury and we went to the cathedral. We lit candles and we spoke to a priest named Rex. He was so warm and kind. Places of worship are often welcoming, warm places – places that allow you to feel a sense of belonging (be it for a short space of time). Every place of worship has its own character and congregation, rendering it unique. Often, it's a place where you can create authentic and lasting connections.

Once I was praying in Regents Park Mosque. A one-pound coin fell out of my pocket and landed in front of the stranger beside me. After I had finished the prayer, she handed it to me. We began talking. Her name was Maria, she was seventeen years old, she told me she had travelled a long way to arrive at the mosque. She was feeling lost and hopeless and in need of connection. We spoke of the spiritual struggle, of wandering in cemeteries, we spoke of all things intangible and out of this world. We spoke about love and sisterhood. Afterwards my friends showed up at the mosque and I introduced them to her. We all ended up going to South Kilburn artist studios, to an event my sister was hosting. We became close but fleeting friends. A few months later, on a summer's afternoon, we found ourselves wandering around West Norwood Cemetery together. We sat in the colourful walled garden at Brockwell park in silence.

One evening, I found myself in a café with two young Mormon men from Utah, the three of us bought luxury hot chocolates complete with marshmallows and spent an hour discussing faith and God and our experiences. Elder Stradling and Elder Terry were their names, they looked like schoolboys, they wore name badges and were dressed very smartly. We had met on a roadside in Tooting a few days earlier when they were trying to convert me. At the time I would take up any opportunity to talk about faith and signs – conversations that can be sparse and often, difficult and unwanted. Faith grounds us and connects us to each other.

Faith and community often go hand in hand. I first experienced being part of a community at Goldsmiths. I became close to the girls at the Islamic Society. We would eat together, pray together, play football, seek religious knowledge, and support one another on our path. It was a sisterhood that was both nourishing and supportive. I will always remember Goldsmiths, not as the institution whereby I acquired a degree, but a place where I learnt about my faith and experienced unconditional and lasting love - the love of my sisters in faith. To this day, the women I met at Goldsmiths inspire me and guide me. They're strong, independent, successful Muslim women who have found a way to thrive in their careers and cultivate their creativity whilst holding firmly onto their faith, often embodying it. My time at university was filled with challenges. I suffered from physical and mental illness - faith gave me the courage to keep going against all odds. The prayer room was my refuge and sanctuary.

When I worked at an Age Activity Centre, which was mostly frequented by Caribbean elders, I found they were often bound together by their church and their faith. Every Wednesday a choir mistress would lead the elders in singing songs of devotion. The members would often bless one another. I felt inspired and as though, even though I was so different, that I belonged. Sometimes I would sing songs of devotions with them, during the last song we would all hold hands. The song would end with the words 'go in peace, go in faith, go in love.' I attended a funeral when one of the elders passed away. The church service was beautiful and humbling - filled with tears and songs and laughter. Many of the elders came. We embraced. Faith connects us in deep and often mysterious ways. It provides us with loving connections.

Over the years I've developed so many strong connections with unlikely people, our love is rooted in our faith. One of my closest friends is an older Ghanaian woman who I see as a mother figure. She worked as a chef at the Age Activity Centre. She always made me feel a sense of belonging. She would encourage me to pray and seek peace with God at times when my life was falling apart, and she was the only person I could talk to. She made me feel part of her family. I met her daughters and her husband, and they showed me such kindness. They invited me into their home. We ate and danced together.

Religious spaces are often beautiful and interesting in and of themselves – but our unique experiences of them render them more so. I've explored breathtaking places of worship across the world; the Sistine Chapel, the Umayyad masjid in Damascus, Notre Dame, Bulguksa Temple in Gyeongju. Yet, it's always the smaller lesser-known places of worship that I find more interesting. A tiny mosque in Melbourne. A church filled with clowns in Hoxton. A mandir molded from sandstone in Alperton. The countless places of worship in London - the mosque I go to for Friday prayers with my dad in Morden.

Religious spaces and signs can act as portals, transporting us to other worlds and heightening our levels of consciousness. I once visited Suleymaniye in Hackney. The mosque was beautiful, salmon pink, so pink, and ottoman-esque. On the edge of the prayer space, there was a creche, and some boards propped up against a corner. I poked my head between two and peered in. On the floor, there were aging and young Turkish women sat cross-legged, kneading dough. One caught my eye and smiled at me, a kind smile and so I smiled back. I went into the quiet prayer space and prayed, and then after I prayed I went outside the room near the kitchen and ate my sandwiches. A young lady around my age came out and joined me. She asked if I lived in the area and told me the women were making sweet dishes for a celebration on Friday. She said that I should come. I said I would try and then an older woman called her and she left.

I went back into the prayer space and sat alone again, smiling as I thought about all those women chatting in Turkish and kneading dough, and all those children laughing and playing. The mosque felt so warm and lived in, and I got that feeling I would often get when I was at a Turkish mosque in Dalston as I often was, surrounded by Turkish people talking in Turkish, maybe that feeling was a bittersweet loneliness... or apartness and longing, but it soon left me and I began to say another prayer, there on that salmon carpet.

My explorations around London's spaces of worship are filled with stories and experiences of human kindness and generosity. I once took a friend, Robbie, a wanderer and a writer, to New Peckham Mosque. It was housed in a Grade 1 listed church. Maghrib prayers had ended and the mosque was rather empty. The chandeliers hung down from the great big ceiling. The imam was still there. He approached us with a smile and showed us around the mosque. He was down to earth and kind. It was Robbie's first time entering into a mosque and he found it to be a fascinating warm space. It's interesting and very encouraging to enable people access to spaces they feel are not for them – and for them to experience a sense of belonging for a brief while in those spaces, however fractured that sense of belonging may be.

I love talking to people about faith and hearing about their ideas and thoughts. Often I take people to Aziziye Mosque in Dalston on my tours. I've watched as women's eyes fill with tears at the sound of the adhaan, the call to prayer – women from different backgrounds and walks of life. They often ask many questions and express how beautiful and uplifting and strange it is to witness the act of prayer. Sometimes they comment on the pureness of the energy. Often, it's people's first time visiting a mosque, or a mandir or a temple.

Sometimes the symbols and signs of faith come from unexpected places. One afternoon, I was wandering around Bunhill Cemetery with a friend. It was an overcast, nowhere November's day. I noticed the tomb of John Bunyan, a body made of stone - his eyes were covered in moss, and there was a pigeon perched on his face. Later I read up on him and I came by some words that he wrote in 'Pilgrim's Progress' which made my heart almost stop; *"I will stay in prison till the moss grows on my eyelids rather than disobey God."* I've also been inspired by the findings of Nicola White, a mudlark guide friend. She had collected so many religious effigies embedded in mud that had been washed up on the Thames shore. She had collected letters in bottles, a few were addressed to God. She spoke of messages coming to her at certain points in her life. We once led a group wandering together, she brought along with her all sorts of things she'd found that told so many stories, or parts of stories.

As a guide, I feel like it's a part of my work to guide people towards the parts of themselves that they may have forgotten about, to offer opportunities to see things differently, and to draw attention to the miracles that manifest in the every day, the way that countless guides have done for me. I'm so interested in the ways faith draws us to each other and shapes the narratives that make up our lives.

Safety

"Wherever you go, there you are" – Thomas a Kempis

I've often found myself in dangerous situations – I once found myself trapped by the seashore at the foot of a cliff, the tide was rising. I once found myself with a friend on her sailboat at night, in the freezing cold, the fuel had run out and we were stuck in the harbour. I once saw a crowd of wild horses running towards me. I once found myself wandering down a nameless path in empty fields, twilight looming, and OS map in hand. Once, in Ayubia, the mountains of Pakistan, my sisters, my dad and I, heard a mountain lion at the window of our shabby guest room on a winter's night. I've walked in remote areas. I've walked in haunted grounds and through ghostly forests, and braved ditches, motorcycle gangs, and narrow paths shrouded in thorns.

    I remember exploring edgelands on the outskirts of cities and traversing unlikely spaces - a river, home to colourful and trippy boathouses by the Shoreham coast, the wild and baron heathland of Dunwich on a foggy day, the empty shacks of Dungeness. I remember the long journeys to get to nowhere landscapes, remote and otherworldly, Snape Maltings, Canvey Island, Gravesend, Poulruan, Romney Marshes, Blakeney, Formby.

    Sometimes whilst walking in nowhere spaces, along canals and rivers and country paths, I feel the presence of others (celestial and earthly). I remember walking along the Old Saxon Shore one day, by the estuary of the Thames. The landscape felt otherworldly, there were horses and no people. The land was flat, the sky was big, I climbed up onto the flat concrete roof plain of a disused artillery fort covered in coloured spray paint. There were some cows in a neighbouring field, the wind blew, and the waters of the estuary moved slowly. There were bits of trash by the shore.

It felt like I was the only person alive in a post-apocalyptic world. I also felt inexplicably uneasy - as though I was being watched. I remember feeling the same way whilst walking through empty bushland and by the East Sea at dawn.

In all these situations, I've sought comfort and solace in Allah, in reciting invocations, in praying for guidance and protection. God has always protected me and saved me in times of need when I've felt most small and vulnerable. These are the times I've most felt God's presence; when close to danger, when reminded of my mortality and the fragility of life. It renders you humble, and meek - but also resilient. I've always been one to take the path less travelled.

I believe God is closest to you at the pinnacle of desperation and misery, and height of joy and wonderment. I once swam in the sea at sunrise in Cetara, Italy, with my sister after fajr prayers. The water was warm and the landscape otherworldly and beautiful. Moments of bliss, in which you're reunited with a loved one that you haven't seen in forever, in those moments I feel closest to God. When you can articulate nothing, but rather must simply let go, to experience and to feel, truly feel alive.

Struggle

"It takes courage... to endure the sharp pains of self-discovery rather than choose to take the dull pain of unconsciousness that would last the rest of our lives." — Marianne Williamson

My journey of faith has been marked with difficulties – throughout my life, I have endured periods of confusion and loss. Many times, I have lost myself. I have abandoned my values, my ideals, my dreams, my faith. I've fallen short a thousand times over in my pursuit to find lasting peace and to live a good and godly life. The pursuit in itself has always felt out of reach – beyond me. Having faith and committing to the spiritual path is not easy, it is exhausting and never-ending. I'm at constant war with myself. Often, I've wondered what would happen if I threw in the towel, abandoned the path, and started again, down a different path. But there are only two paths, one towards God and one away from Him. Somehow I've never gone too far down the road away from God. Something always draws me back, like gravity. Once you've experienced the magic of faith, when you've been saved innumerable times, given a thousand chances to start over, and experienced the clarity and deep love that comes with cultivating a relationship with God, you realise nothing else will fill you with that same peace.

Being a guide has taught me resilience. It has taught me to see a path to its end, to brave all weathers, to endure with grace, each trial and difficulty – to never cease to seek guidance, or be afraid to go back if you take a wrong turn. Life presents you constantly with choices that lead you closer or further away. I've always felt at war with my lower self – a self that often self-sabotages, that hurts others, that can be reckless, dark and detached, and that seeks solace through dangerous means. We are all one choice away from a completely different life – and too often, I have been close to choosing a life that I know will cause me to suffer. And the ultimate suffering is being cut off from God. In Islam, the ninety-nine names of Allah are so revealing and reverent. Allah – the Guide, the Most Kind, the Subtle One, the Opener of Doors, the Restorer, the Bestower of Mercy.

Often faith presents you with new ways of seeing. It takes you out of the world, to a place abundant with miracles, epiphanies, mystery, and wonder. It causes you to see beauty and connection manifest and to experience synchronicity that draws you closer to your Creator. Sometimes, it overwhelms you - it finds you in unexpected places and it awakens you- Taqwa – God-consciousness. During one Ramadan I found myself at Glastonbury. One of my best friends Aisha, a talented journalist, was hosting a discussion at Left Field and I promised her I would go with her. I made the promise before I unexpectedly left London for Australia. It was whilst in Australia, I faced trials that brought me closer to Allah. I spent a lot of time reading scriptures, seeking solace in mosques and empty spaces like St Kilda's beach or the bushland. I returned on a spiritual high, and I regretted that I had made the promise to go to the music festival.

It was one of the muddiest and wettest year at Glastonbury. My friend and I camped out in the Left Field. On the evening we arrived, we hiked up a hill with a pad Thai takeaway we had bought from a stall, we watched the sunset and opened our fasts. It was surreal and dreamlike. We would wake up for sehri, eat by the campfire, and pray before heading back to our tent. The fasts were long and difficult. We were seeking spiritual purification, all around us people were smoking pot and drinking and partying. We would drift around in dungarees and wellies.

I love music. We went to see many of my favourite musicians, Lapsley and Tame Impala. At times I would sing along to headline acts at the top of my voice. I would forget myself. Though the experience felt oddly spiritual in itself, remembering God in an unlikely place, praying and feeling a sense of sisterhood and unconditional love towards my friend. We had been through so many odd and beautiful things together over the years, that it felt almost natural that we should share such an experience – strange, paradoxical, reflective of our very existence. I remember one night, having opened our fast, we went to see Muse. The atmosphere was electric. They performed some of my favourite songs, Plug in Baby and Time is Running Out. Then, when they started to play Dead Inside, I felt it. I felt dead inside. I had to get away. I felt so ashamed and apologetic in front of God. I had spent previous months doing everything I could to develop a sense of closeness, and in the holy month, possibly my last Ramadan on earth, I was at Glastonbury.

We learn from our experiences. Sometimes they seek to reaffirm the beliefs we hold close to our hearts. It's only having erred, so many times, in many ways, you see wisdom in divine laws. You realise they're only there to protect you, to make your life easier. Often I wish I could go back in time and undo things, but more often than not, I just pray that I learn from my mistakes, that I can forgive myself and know that, given the chance, I would do things differently – especially when the mistakes involving causing others hurt.

*

The stars are shining in the sky – I wonder, how often do we look up? Last night, I lay on a mungee on the rooftop and counted the stars. I was reminded of how small and insignificant I am, how big and beautiful the universe is – I thought about the everlasting mysteries that shroud all human life and the elusive possibilities that are forever in reach. There is something so grounding about looking at the sky. Since arriving in Lahore, I have watched the sunrise and set from the rooftop many times. I've watched the sky change colour, for me, its therapy – a calming feeling always settles in me. The other evening, my cousin pointed out letters 'Allah' in Arabic floating in the sky, almost slanted but there, written in the clouds.

When I was a child I spent great chunks of time staring at the clouds and talking to God. In recent years, I've felt myself become more and more rooted in earthly pursuits and desires – in making money and seeking to buy a flat and thinking about a future I might never arrive at. There's little space left in my mind, for thoughts of eternity - though my soul longs to go back to nature, to revive spiritual ambitions. These days, while my life has come to an almost standstill, faith - my relationship with God - has been brought to the forefront of my mind. I pray, that I can trust once again in God's plan. To let go of the fear and anxiety that comes with being so rooted in this world – I pray to soar again, in the sky above, endless and magnificent.

On Transience

"The butterfly counts not months but moments, and has time enough." — Rabindranath Tagore

"Dil lagh gya?" Since arriving back in Lahore, I've been asked this question countless times. I translate this to mean, has your heart become attached *or* are you *here* now? My answer is mostly "jee" (yes), or sometimes, "humesha" (always). If there's one thing I've learnt in life, and it's taken a very long time to learn this, it's how to be specifically present in one place at one time. Presence is integral to experience. Without presence, we live lives outside of ourselves, often we cease to live at all. Presence lies at the heart of consciousness. In the past, I have struggled to actualize presence.

Growing up my default way of life and living consisted of absence – emotional, mental, sometimes physical absence. When I was in my early teens I constantly felt like I was living in a dream. I later came to identify with experiencing a dissociative disorder – like derealization or depersonalisation. It was frustrating and equally frightening. I felt like a stranger inside of myself, I felt like I was floating in a dream that wasn't mine. I was never present because I didn't belong to myself. It's a difficult feeling to describe to someone who has never experienced anything similar. Maybe it's owing to the experience, or the lack of experienced authentic presence that made me realize early on, how very transient and fragile life is. How often our lives consist of a few breaths in a few places. A stream of what felt like illusions. It felt like the entire world was made up of paper, and it was one blustery storm away from entirely collapsing. These thoughts and feelings always rendered me inexplicably lonely.

Has my heart become attached? As I've grown older, I've felt more rooted in the world. Now experiences of depersonalisation only come in waves as opposed to a constant undercurrent - often triggered by moments of intensity. Moments like finding myself very ill in Han Noi, or having tea by a mountainside café overlooking Damascus at night or witnessing an especially beautiful sunrise alone by the lonely coast, or experiencing an especially painful parting. Is this life real? I often ask myself. I begin to float again.

Of course, there are a hundred reasons why I could say no. "Nai, mera dil nehi lagh gya." I'm finding it increasingly hard to speak one language and think in another. I don't know what I'm doing here and the more I'm asked about my plans for the future the less clear they seem. The future is but a mirage, in a desert with no name. Nothing is anchoring me here, at the same time there's nowhere I'd rather be. And I feel like an essential part of me is missing. I'm not sure if I'm here now, or if my heart is really attached.

When I was young, and my mum was away in Lahore (she would often go for prolonged periods of time) I wrote a poem pertaining to this feeling, - *ami mere dil is dunya main nehi lag ta*. My heart has not become attached. I don't feel as though I belong in this world. It was a desperately sad poem. It reflected a sense of detachment I had felt my whole life, to both people and place. Though somehow, over the years I have managed to invert that sense of detachment in an almost paradoxical way. I can belong anywhere. There was a power there, in that essential loneliness. And as a guide, it became increasingly important to me to enable and empower others to belong anywhere. I longed for people to feel that their heart could become attached to any place, in an almost alchemical fashion, to turn loneliness and isolation, into a sense of belonging- through love, kindness, and connection.

I've never truly missed anyone. Missing, to me, is an abstract concept and I feel I lack the capabilities to engage with it. Maybe because I come from a family where everyone is constantly coming and going, and that from a young age I learnt to disassociate – as a way of allowing myself to feel peace, a peace that wasn't dependent on anyone human being. Growing up, many of those closest to me moved away, or would go away for long periods of time. We were loved, but we were taught to be emotionally independent and resilient. Every separation I've experienced with a friend, family member, or lover, has since strengthened this sense of dissociation. I've never been able to articulate this in a way that doesn't make me seem like a monster. I am capable of love, but I've learnt to keep going when love is no longer present. When I lose someone, when I find myself far away, I look inwards, I seek refuge in God and myself. I've learned to love for God's sake - this is the purest and truest love I know.

Here, now in Lahore with my mum, I haven't yet called anyone back home. Home feels like a distant dream. It's selfish perhaps, but we've always been self-sufficient and disconnected in our own ways, my mother and I. We've always learnt to keep calm and carry on. In the absence of people, and at times, in the absence of self, there is just an emptiness that remains - nothing more, nothing less – but love is ever-present. The present is the only place I aspire to live in, it's the only place that is livable – to seek beauty in transience, to accept love be it fleeting, to cease to have lengthy hopes – but to hope, always hope, that the light never dies.

Loneliness

"At the innermost core of all loneliness is a deep and powerful yearning for union with one's lost self." — Brendan Francis

It can be a very lonely vocation, being a guide. It's a role that requires you to be open, responsive, and very patient. It can also, at times, make you feel quite isolated. Over the last few years, I have led many tours and excursions for large groups of English language students, groups of Italians, Koreans, Argentinians, Ukrainians, Brazilians, Dutch – you slowly pick up things very specific to an individual culture and you also find yourself, very often, entirely lost in translation. And then you would have more mixed groups which were always more fun. Sometimes work didn't feel at all like work. It felt like going to the theatre to see a musical with friends, or going for a wander around the museum, having lunch together in a restaurant in Oxford or Cambridge. Often you find yourself waiting alone outside churches and museums and coach stations for the group to come back on time, and praying silently that they do.

I once received a commission from an English language school I was working with jointly with the Bank of Georgia to deliver a programme of social excursions and activities. Three extraordinary young people had been awarded an opportunity to leave the Georgian Mountains where they lived, and travel to London for a few weeks to study English. The young woman was studying nursing and worked as a shepherdess. The young man brewed tea using mountain herbs, and the second young man weaved baskets by hand which he flogged on mountainside roads. I spent the better part of two weeks with them - we visited places that were specific to their interests, like the Twinings Tea Museum and the Petrie Museum of Egyptian Archaeology.

On the first day of their visit, we were joined by a Georgian filmmaker and an interpreter - both were very lovely and were able to converse with the students in their mother tongue. The following two weeks were exhausting, revealing, and quite lonely. They spoke very limited English. I almost felt like I was a teenager again. I felt like a peer and an outsider. I made changes to the programme often, we ate street food by the canal in Camden, hiked up Primrose Hill, went to Notting Hill. I spoke in simple sentences and we often communicated using signs and body language.

One day they arrived late at our meeting point, our train was subsequently delayed. We made it to Victoria coach station three minutes after the coach had departed for Cambridge. I felt deflated and done. Instead, I decided we would go to Brighton. It took more than two hours because of works on the train line. Upon arriving, they asked me when we would be going to Cambridge, not quite understanding that we had missed the coach. It was exhausting. It was a sunny day. We sat in a greasy spoon along the promenade. They didn't like the fish and chips and I suggested we enjoy some free time and meet up afterwards. They agreed. I sat by the sea and wondered about my life choices.

I came to really like them. I got to know them mostly through their interactions with each other. The three of them went from being strangers to becoming very close friends. I think the young lady and one of the young men had become more than friends towards the end of the trip. On the last day, I gave them gifts and bid them farewell. One of the young men told me to come to Georgia one day and that he would be my guide. I smiled and said maybe. It's a request guides receive so very often. I wondered if they understood how much I had given them of myself – as tour guides, we often go above and beyond to make others feel comfortable and taken care of, sometimes to our own detriment – but we move, we push through with grace and humility and gratitude. Being a guide is so much more than a job.

I've been in similar situations. I once led a bespoke tour for a group of inspirational Swedish women, a couple of whom couldn't speak much English. It was hard to figure out whether or not they were enjoying the tour. I made an effort to speak slowly, to simplify stories and insights. Where I can, I try to make my tours as visually interesting and experiential as possible. I realized, having led more and more tours - that the most important thing is that people have a good time, enjoy themselves, see new sights and share new experiences. That's why often food has been integral to my favourite tours. The ability to sit in a local café, eat and talk, is so invaluable. Being a guide, you see vulnerabilities in others, you begin to question your lifestyle and life choices - you have countless others' lives to compare it too. The opportunities you are presented with are both life-affirming and paralyzing – there are so many choices and ways to exist.

As a guide, often you can be whoever you want to be, you can put on a personality – it takes you out of the mundane drudgery of everyday life into the magical world of possibilities – each experience is a reminder to yourself and to others that life is big, and the possibilities to explore and connect are endless. It's never too late to return to our childlike states of innocence, curiosity, and wonder. Every wandering offers an opportunity to share beliefs and talk honestly about real things, like death and loss, religion, politics, the meaning of life. The spaces we traverse act as prompts - the cemetery, the community garden – walls come tumbling down and you experience a fleeting sense of intimacy. It's sometimes one that I've not experienced with lifelong friends and family members. There's a kind of security that comes with knowing that you will probably never see someone again – that in itself can also make you feel quite lonely.

There are different kinds of loneliness. Sometimes loneliness can be beautiful, tinged with a sweet sorrow it can make you feel more alive. Other times it can make you feel powerless and turn your insides black.

Throughout my life, I've often had to process things alone. I've gone through my darkest moments, my most intense heartbreaks and breakdowns alone, as well as through illuminating breakthroughs and epiphanies that clarify. I've found a sense of resilience and self-sufficiency in this, and power, of owning much of my life, of not giving things away in a society in which we give everything away – in which we allow strangers windows into our more private lives. I've learnt that it's good to have boundaries and to protect yourself by keeping certain things to yourself. I've learnt to protect my dreams and to leave my disappointments unvoiced. In practicing self-preservation, you become more secure in yourself and more authentic in your actions, they're founded on purer intentions. You learn to find meaning in your own stories and life lessons. You discover a peace within yourself. You find a home within yourself. Our answers are rarely found outside ourselves.

All things are fleeting and temporary, the highest of highs and the lowest of lows – everything will pass. I've realized that no one can save you. I used to feel so bitter and angry at different times in my life. I felt like no one had the answers and cures that I sought. No one understood. But the more you let go, the more you realise that you have to do things for yourself and the only one you can call on is God, the more peace becomes you.

You also appreciate connection so much more – you appreciate the people you can talk to and confide in, the people who you understand and who understand you. Those people occupy a special place in your heart. You realise also that that feeling of home, of familiarity and warmth, comes from people to whom you feel connected. They make foreign places feel like your childhood stomping grounds - familiar and comfortable. While I was in Korea, my best friend whom I love unconditionally never allowed me to feel like an outsider. I felt a sense of relief in being the other. In other cities, where I felt no great sense of connection or love, I felt so alone. I'd feel the most alone while I was eating out – whilst having a pizza in a Somali café, or seafood pancake in a Korean restaurant - alone. I understand my clients because I've been in their shoes. Often when I'm leading a tour for a lady who's travelling solo, I understand why she would love to spend a bit more time together at the end of a tour – to have a coffee or walk a little further. It's often owing to a sense of loneliness. My tours often run over. I often allow them too.

Vulnerability

"Everyone's alone — or so it seems to me. They make noises, and think they are talking to each other; They make faces and think they understand each other. And I'm sure they don't. Is that a delusion?" — T.S. Eliot

Being a renegade guide, you're often quite vulnerable. Sometimes you find yourself discussing your innermost thoughts and beliefs, things both serious and absurd. Sometimes you laugh together, rarely you cry together. You become very aware of the transient nature of your time together. It makes honest conversation easy, and sometimes this is one of my favourite aspects of my job. You can let your guard down and talk about things without fear of judgment or longevity – there's no need for follow up questions further on down the line or elongated explanations to complicated feelings. You develop new ways of seeing a particularly perplexing issue, and sometimes you're provided with an answer that never crossed your mind.

    I remember once at the end of a tour, I went to eat with one of my guests, Olivia. She was a lovely Australian East Asian lady, maybe a couple of years younger than me. We ended up discussing relationships. She had fallen for a Syrian man in Turkey and they were currently in a long-distant relationship. She would have to overcome a lot of obstacles to be with him. We talked at length about the value of love and about what truly matters. At the time, I was seeing someone I could envision a future with; a kind, spirited, and loving man. He happened to be an undocumented migrant and recently our relationship was becoming strained. I wanted to be with him, but I didn't know if I could, if I was committed or in love enough. Whether I could make the sacrifices I knew our love would entail. I felt conflicted, and awful. I was constantly overcome by guilt and uncertainty.

Olivia told me she was visiting the man she loved every few months in Turkey, while living and working in London. She was going against the advice given by her friends and family. She had decided to fight - to put aside cultural and religious differences to be with the man she loved, a Muslim man. We said our goodbyes at the end of the meal and embraced - we were no longer strangers.

I wondered whether it would work out for her, and for me. I wondered what was wrong with me, and why I had never fought for anything the way she had and that rendered me quite sad. Maybe I didn't understand the true meaning of love and sacrifice. Because every time I had been in a situation similar to hers (or a situation that required a great deal of sacrifice) I would eventually give up. I kept in touch with Olivia. I watched her journey unfold over the years via Instagram stories and posts. She moved to Turkey and she married him - they lived beautiful lives - and it made me so happy. The people I meet inspire me endlessly. They help me to realise that pretty much anything is possible. They give me permission to do things differently, to take risks, to know that the outcomes may well be worth it.

On some occasions, I'm required to act the role of a textbook tour guide. To provide information, access, and stories. Sometimes, the people I tour for can be so passive and difficult – on those occasions I'm reminded that this is a job, even though for me it's so much more than a job.

I once led a tour for an American family. It was a very uncomfortable experience. The family was quiet and they seemed to be experiencing domestic issues. I felt like I was right in the middle of it. They seemed to be uncomfortable with my presence as a young brown woman and tour giver. The first question the dad asked me was "Do you need a license to guide?" I've been asked this question many times. Usually I don't mind and I'll answer honestly.

But it was the tone in which he said it, it was patronizing and unpleasant.

I got to discover more and more about them on the tour. His wife was a petite Asian woman, he met her at a wedding and his stepdaughter lived in London with her partner. Her partner had lived in the area in which I was leading the tour for many years. The stepdaughter and her partner were quiet throughout. I figured maybe they were just a bit socially awkward or uninterested. I tried to do my best to stay positive and to stick to the script. (I didn't have a script). It was a night tour. The high street was unusually quiet. We ate samosas outside Pooja. The mint chutney fell on my clothes. I spotted some of my old classmates, they eyed me suspiciously. I felt like I was in a sitcom, 'Bad Guide' maybe. I looked ridiculously out of place among them. I made an extra effort. I introduced them to people I knew in the area, in the markets and shops.

The last stop was going to be Springfield, the ground of a psychiatric hospital, but I had decided that it probably wasn't safe to visit by night. I didn't realise that due to daylight savings, it would be dark when I ran the tour. I was at fault. I recommended some local restaurants to them and bid them farewell. I had a feeling they would leave a bad review and they did. It was the first bad review I had ever received in all my years of touring. I felt sad and a bit angry. I was angry that I introduced them to friends and told them personal stories and took them to special places in my area that even locals didn't know about. I led another similar tour the next day. It was for two Italian sisters; they were both nice enough but they were very quiet and it was hard to decipher whether or not they were enjoying themselves. I tried to find out what interested them in life, in hopes I could share information and stories that were relevant to them, but it proved difficult and soon I just stopped trying so hard. When you get nothing back, it's exhausting.

After that, I decided I no longer wanted to run wandering experiences by night for small groups. The pay was minimal, and for some reason, they were becoming more joyless. Being a guide, you put so much of yourself into what you do, you try so hard to make everyone feel happy and comfortable and when they don't, you feel rejected. Fortunately, I have very few experiences such as these. My skin has grown thicker and I have had to remind myself it's a job – I'm providing a service and not everyone will always be interested and interesting. It's a lesson I had already learnt the hard way when I first started out, but relearning it after so many years was difficult. It's personal, as a guide, it always feels personal and it hurts when you're made to feel small and vulnerable.

Goodbyes

"It's the emptiest and yet the fullest of all human messages: 'Good-bye." — Kurt Vonnegut

It's close to midnight, the rain is pouring down, lightning spreads unevenly across the sky and thunderous booms reverberate in this echoic home. Soon, I will be leaving Lahore. I will once again have to say goodbye to the city and my loved ones. The thought of having to say goodbye once again to my cousins who I've grown so close to in a short space of time, makes me feel immensely miserable.

    I've always been really bad at saying goodbye. I'll often opt to say nothing at all. Goodbyes mark an end, maybe I've sometimes been unable to acknowledge an end because I felt like I was never really there in the first place. I guess it comes back to that sense of separateness. I think it was the last day of secondary school when I realised how little the place meant to me, how unattached I was from it all; the hallways, the canteens, the corridors, my teachers and my friends. Five years at the same school and I was indifferent to the fact that it was over. The announcement was made on the loudspeaker - we were free to go! I remember the noise and the excitement of it all, the sound of my classmates cheering and shouting. As everyone poured out of the classroom and towards the field, I quietly slipped through the fire exit and made my way home via the shortcut through the mental hospital. I never said goodbye to anyone, I just left. While others made their memories and took their photos and signed each other's jumpers I decided to walk the path of the stranger. I ended up going to the local park and there I set my uniform on fire, it felt great! I did get some closure in the end. It's always been that way. I've always looked inwards from the fringes. The path of the stranger can be a lonely one to tread sometimes.

It was much the same at college, only rather than appreciating the freedom of being alone like I had done before, now I longed for company, for true friendship, I think. The flitters were no longer enough, people who came in and out of my life for brief periods. I felt a deep sense of loneliness that led to a depression that wouldn't lift, even when I tried counselling. I would have to search deep down within my soul for answers.

I never said goodbye when I left college. I never said goodbye when I left my part-time job at the pharmacy. I never said goodbye to the children at the centre I worked at or the refugee drop-in where I worked. I never said goodbye to my classmates at pottery or BSL or stained glass. Endings have always been abrupt and fractured. I never said goodbye to Chanmi when she left London. I never said goodbye to university. I never went to my graduation. I graduated a year late and everyone I knew had already left by then. Sometimes I think that things are best left unsaid, that life is a continuation and that you'll meet those you're meant to meet again, and that places will come up again.

Things change, we learn, we grow. As a guide and community worker, I have learnt the importance of saying goodbye, in voicing the words and relaying the sentiments. Though sometimes, they're elongated, fractured, ridiculous, drawn-out, and incomplete. You learn to meet people where they are, to say goodbye in a way that is kind and befitting.

Goodbyes are especially difficult if you genuinely connected with a community, group, or individual. I've gotten so much better at saying goodbye, with grace and love – at the community canteens where I worked, I made a point to say goodbye to every individual I had gotten to know. At the Age Activity Centre, I gave out gifts and made a speech (with much difficulty) reminding the elders how special they are, and how much that inspired and moved me. Afterwards a few of the hard of hearing elders wished me happy birthday to which I told them, it wasn't my birthday, I was leaving. One of my favourite elders made a speech and we all held hands and embraced, and I left heartbroken but whole, humbled, and contented. Our connections will always live on in some form, be it through our memories, our stories or our exchanges with eternity. Every goodbye leaves us a little emptier and a little fuller.

*

Life is transient, people come and go. Nothing is promised to us, at least for the duration of our earthly stay. Though the thought makes me sad, it is also comforting. In my life, I change jobs often, I come and go, some of my closest friends and family members live across oceans and often have drifted away. But life moves on and we must move with it, otherwise we risk being left behind and we risk never moving at all. The more we come to terms with this truth, that life is so fleeting and that will never live a moment again, the more we learn to live wholly, to be more appreciative of what we have when we have it, of the conversations we share, the love we receive and the good that comes to us. Transience makes it easier to forgive, and harder to hold on to hate. Being a guide has taught me how to walk away, to say goodbye, and to feel a sense of deep gratitude for every encounter - for every person that enriches my soul and shows me kindness. We learn to pay it forward.

    The time will come, too soon, for me to say goodbye to Lahore once more - to family and friends that I have come to know and love all over again. The most painful and difficult goodbyes are always those I share with my family in Lahore. They're so heartbreaking, that it makes me not want to leave. *Nai Jao.* Don't Go. When these words were communicated to me, by someone who is closest to me spiritually than anyone else in the world, my heart hurt so much I could hardly breathe. I don't want to say goodbye. I don't want to leave - and that is the tragedy of being a stranger – of living a broken fragmented life, of belonging everywhere and nowhere. But we move.

On Love

"When we love, we always strive to become better than we are. When we strive to become better than we are, everything around us becomes better too." — Paulo Coelho

There's no place in the world where I have experienced love in the way I have in Lahore. It is a love that runs deep – a love that simultaneously heals and fractures, protects and suffocates. It permeates into every interaction and encounter. I learnt the meaning of love, universal and pure, on a previous visit to Lahore. It was the first time I discovered the true value of family, friendship, and community. It's where I experienced my first heartbreak.

I used to believe that there were essentially different kinds of love - romantic love, platonic love, familial love. I used to subscribe to a belief system that valued romantic love about all other kinds of love. But I no longer believe in the hierarchy and separation that exists between different kinds of love. Apart from the love of God, all other kinds of love run parallel and are capable of changing us for the better. Being a guide has taught me so much about love.

I've learnt through the connections I've formed, through the couples I have met, many of whom have inspired me with their unwavering commitment to one another and to jointly making the world a more loving place. I've learnt from the seekers of love that I meet. Love is a topic that comes up again and again in conversation whilst on wandering tours - people divulge personal stories, the struggles that fractured past relationships, their ongoing search for a soul mate. People from all backgrounds and walks of life, people who are confident, beautiful, and successful, are often lonely. They share what they desire and voice their fears. There's something freeing about having honest conversations about love with complete strangers.

Often these conversations have caused me to look inwards and to revisit my past, to reflect on love stories that occupy hidden spaces in my mind.

More recently, I've relearned the value of self-love. Self-love is one of the most important and difficult loves to reconcile ourselves with. Our most lasting relationship is the one we have with ourselves. To reflect, to forgive ourselves repeatedly, to address our more toxic patterns of behavior and most troubling idiosyncrasies is something that we are all forced to do. To learn to speak to yourself lovingly, to treat yourself well and kindly, to cease to hurt yourself, and to be your own worst enemy. It takes so much work, and persistence to not give up on ourselves. We have to learn to truly love ourselves – and to love ourselves enough to want better. I've spent so much of my life at war with myself, constantly angry and disappointed in myself for the things I did and didn't do, the things I said and didn't say, the person I was and the person I could never be. It's only through slowly beginning to love myself, and becoming my own best friend, that I learnt that I could do and, more essentially, *be* better.

The older you get the more friends you lose and the more you value the people who have stuck around. It's so important to surround yourself with people who are grateful and appreciative of life and beauty, who respect you and speak to you with kindness. People who love you and who you love back. We lose patience with those who constantly hurt us, belittle us, who make our lives harder. My closest remaining friends are those who share similar values, who have pure hearts, who possess kindness and warmth and a sense of humour. The closest people to me, have always been my parents and my sisters, Sofia and Noreen. They have continually inspired me with their authenticity, loyalty, kindness, creativity, and humility. Familial love is a sacred and lasting love – it is a love that is unconditional, that challenges you, pushes you, helps you to grow.

Being a guide presents me with opportunities to practice being a more loving and patient person. I read a book called 'A Return to Love' by Marianne Williamson. It resonated with me. She emphasized the importance of channeling love into everything you do, in your work and interactions. Love in its truest form is the love of God, and it is this love I seek to express subconsciously, and always. Love, I believe, can heal us and others. It can make everything around us better.

Romantic Love

**"The love we had in our past, unfinished, untested, lost love, seems so easy, so childish to those of us who choose to settle down. But, actually, it's the purest, most concentrated stuff."
— Modern Love Stories**

The few times I've fallen in love, my experiences have been intense, elusive, and fraught with difficulties. I've experienced strange and beautiful love stories marked with magic and synchronicity and often ending in tragedy. Growing up, I was always a hopeless romantic. I was always in love with the idea of love – a love that is beautiful, healing, and restorative. I dreamed of marrying someone I could share my life with and vice versa.

I've always been drawn to special individuals. Individuals who have taught me so much about myself, life, and love. The best love stories, I believe, aren't always the ones with happy endings, but the ones that help us to truly grow, to learn more about ourselves, and to teach us lessons that we will never forget. Many of my stories involve guiding or are intrinsic to my journey towards being a guide. Nothing quite guides us and instructs us like love, nothing takes us down so many stretching roads, dark alleyways, dead ends, and narrowing gullies, across green plains and endless fields, over rugged mountains, than love. Love has built me and broken me so many times over. It's caused my heart to grow cold and hard, and soft and warm.

Love has always felt somewhat visible, but just out of reach. One of my favourite films, 'Before Sunrise', spoke to me in so many ways, as a dreamer, an idealist, and a guide. I felt like I had lived a version of that story. To meet a stranger, to share a conversation, to explore a city, to fall in love, and to recognize that magic exists. That chance encounters are meaningful beyond measure.

I've often loved the wrong person in the right ways and the right person in the wrong ways. I've loved too little and too much. I've placed my hopes and desires in soulmates only for them to disappear, or for me to disappear. Love has mostly been abrupt and disrupting. I always find love at the wrong time. My heart attaches itself to those it knows it cannot be with. Too often, love has abandoned me, or I have abandoned it. The few times love has seemed in reach, I self-sabotage. Sometimes, I think I'm difficult to love. I'm evasive and noncommittal, I busy myself with external things. I try to save those I love (I'm always drawn to troubled souls), but I end up hurting them and hurting myself. The idea of being anchored to a life, of bearing children, of being tied down – has always terrified me. I wonder if that fear ever goes away, if we're ever ready to commit to another human being for the rest of our lives.

I've become comfortable with the idea of being alone, but I still long for companionship, for a lasting union – one that is healing and enriching, that doesn't leave me broken. That doesn't leave me grappling. Sometimes I feel like the love stories I have lived have been enough for me, provided me with enough romance, and enough friendship and enough life, for me to live off of. I seek comfort in the memories I've shared with those I once loved, wandering around derelict factories and singing sad country songs, sitting by a river and drinking tea, sitting on a rooftop under the stars talking about life and death and everything in between, watching a sunset, watching the moonrise, praying together, wandering together, sharing dreams, creating a private imaginary future in which we could live. I have a lot of beautiful memories that I will never forget. Sometimes, these memories bring me peace and sometimes they bring me sadness. I've lived more for moments of clarity, love, and peace than make-believe happy-ever-afters.

Sometimes I wish I could go back in time and pray to God to guide my relationships, and enable me to get closer to Him through them. Yet, I appreciate every person in my story. I'm old fashioned, my stories have always involved me writing letters or long emails or poems, sharing thoughts and ideas. Communication offers a deep sense of intimacy and connection. To be able to think things through and articulate them wholly has seemed intrinsic to love, and love in its truest form has many purposes.

I've always felt a strong desire to be loved by others. I've always sought to be accepted and embraced for who I am, to always show off my best side, the light in my soul, and not the darkness that often covers it. I've also sought to be charismatic and funny and playful and warm, and whoever I felt someone wanted me to be. It took me a very long time to develop the courage to be disliked. To realise that I can come as I am and that I don't have to try so hard.

Here in Lahore, I find myself praying for guidance, to leave those I love in a better state then I found them, or not leave them at all. I pray for a love that is unconditional, that heals more than it hurts. I pray for a love that is not elusive and destined to end in heartbreak. I pray that I can be open to receiving love – that I do not run away or disappear when it expresses itself.

Dating

"I see myself forever and ever as the ridiculous man, the lonely soul, the wanderer, the restless frustrated artist, the man in love with love, always in search of the absolute, always seeking the unattainable." — Henry Miller

Dating as a guide can be very difficult. Sometimes I don't know when I'm being a guide or when I'm being myself. Sometimes I can't decipher between the two personas. Being a guide requires you to be on. It is a highly performative role, one that requires much energy. You often have to be attentive and to lead on conversations. As a guide, I'm sometimes stood up. I'm asked awkward personal questions. I find myself reluctant to date in my free time. I'd much rather read or write or go for a swim or stare into space. I often feel like my ideal partner would be someone who doesn't talk too much, who I can share silence with – who I can be my least performative self around. Someone who can love and accept me for who I am underneath it all. I don't often let people see me.

    Being a guide has almost paradoxically made dating harder. I'm constantly meeting intelligent interesting people and sharing meaningful conversations, so when I do go on a date, I find it hard to engage in small talk. I much prefer meeting people in real life. Fate, God, has continually brought the most wondrous people my way. I've met people through my explorations, my tours, through my work and written words. I'm a believer in serendipity, but shared journeys have always ended too soon. At times when I find myself lonely, I've resorted to dating apps. On occasion, I've met interesting men through these apps, men who although weren't for me have, like the guests on my tours, inspired me. I've met adventurers, philosophers, and accountants, people I may never have met through any other means. The dates themselves can be enjoyable enough. Often a guy will ask me if I can take him on a tour around London, show him the sights upon finding out what I do. Sometimes I do, and I relay facts and stories on the way. I find it fun. Other times I find it exhausting. Sometimes I don't want to play the guide, I'd rather have tea somewhere ordinary and impersonal, someplace like Café Nero or Costa, but the guide in me is ever accommodating, ever wanting to share something magical.

As a guide and community worker, you never know who you'll meet and that's part of what makes it so interesting. Love can find you, in unexpected ways, and being a guide makes it easier – there are so many places love can find you. My friends often wonder why I haven't met anyone when I meet so many people. I don't try to explain myself. I do meet a lot of people – a German race car driver asks to go dancing and exchange life stories after a tour, a Saudi Arabian man pays for your meal and checks in on you every year, an intelligent Polish poet shares his poetry with you, his love for literature and art. You talk, you share, you explore – an evening trip at an art show in Chelsea, a wander around a conservatory, a walk beside the river. Everyone possesses an intrinsic beauty that seeps into the soul. But I don't fall in love easily, and I've become averse to the idea of falling in love – I don't have the propensity for heartbreak – it always takes a toll on my business, my ability to do my work, and on my mental health. I lack the patience required for love, and I've grown so tired of not being able to return the love I receive – I've grown weary of rejecting good souls and being rejected.

I meet a lot of couples. My Secret Garden wandering in particular is very popular among couples. I once collaborated with a storyteller friend Vanessa, our walk ended in a temple under the stars in Hyde Park. Vanessa told a story, a Greek tragedy. It was a cold night, we sat on the floor and couples shared blankets. I've discovered so many beautiful and whole love stories that make me happy. I met a couple very early on in my touring career, a German couple, they were both kind, compassionate, curious - you could tell their relationship was founded on true love. They would come to many of my tours and even came to my 30th birthday party. They were so supportive. Theirs wasn't a relationship based on ownership but on mutual respect. On one walk, it was only the three of us, and my friend and intern Imogen. I met Imogen at one of my wanderings, a beautiful spirited young woman, who would often come along to recces and on wanderings.

    I've led private walks for many couples. I led a walk for an older lesbian couple in Streatham. One of the women's parents were visiting from Finland and they wanted to show them around the area they had recently moved too. The father of the Finnish woman was a professor, he was very intelligent and a well-known academic - his wife was also well-read. They had been together for over forty years, they had travelled the world together and the love between them was still so strong. The love between the two women also felt so solid. At the end of the walk, I joined the family for tea and cake at the Rookery Café. I felt happy to be part of their story, albeit for a very brief and unlikely time.

    I've led walks for those on a first date. I've led walks for friends who I knew deep down harboured romantic feelings towards one another. Sometimes I became friends with the couples I connected with. I met a couple from America, who moved to my local area and attended my Tooting Tour. The man, Jesse, was a software engineer at Facebook and offered me free Facebook advertising for my tours. He was interested in photography and community. His wife Michelle had lived in Baltimore for a time and was interested in stories of elders, she was once mentored by a senior figure at the NRA (National Rifle Association). We spoke of the importance of speaking and listening to people whose ideas and values are so different from our own, as a way of learning, understanding, and bridging the gap between oppositions. They were both so interesting and kind and made the perfect couple. Months on from the walk, the three of us we met for dinner in a curry house. We shared stories, they gave me advice and encouragement. I felt blessed to know them.

One winter's night I led a tour for a lovely couple, a Chinese woman named Minji, and an Englishman named Paul, in Tooting. Minji had made a name for herself by running authentic walking tours in Chinatown. We chatted animatedly as we went. We chatted about work and journeying and life. As we approached our last stop, the lake at Tooting Common, the couple insisted that I warm up with a cup of jasmine tea at their apartment which was nearby. I relented. Their apartment was beautiful, filled with images and books and relics. They shared with me stories and photographs of their travels. Minji made me tea. They both had very different backgrounds and upbringings, but fell in love and made it work. I could tell just by spending a few hours with them, that they were right for each other - they supported each other and made each other happy.

I've led walks at sunset and twilight, I've seen couples share beautiful moments - watched planes take off and wander the Thames foreshore. Mostly watching these brief moments makes me happy and grateful, but sometimes it heightens my own feelings of disconnection and loneliness. I feel hope in the very idea of love and the possibility of it.

I meet a lot of very inspiring and beautiful single people, some who often express a desire to meet someone. They're often people who are open, adventurous, and very self-aware. A Singaporean PA asks about the best Muslim dating apps in London, a cleaner from Luxemburg expresses a desire to find a long-lost lover, an older independent traveller shares her feelings of loneliness. Sometimes I've felt most alone whilst hearing about the loneliness of others. I wish I could do something. I often wonder about organizing wandering tours for those who are looking for love – there are so many beautiful wondrous lonely souls in the world and it feels wrong that there aren't many meaningful ways for them to connect.

Strange Love

"All living things contain a measure of madness that moves them in strange, sometimes inexplicable ways." — Yann Martel, Life of Pi

Strange love is the love I'm most familiar with. Strange love is a love that can't be categorized, can't be put in a box, or labelled, or explained. It's a love that can't be voiced - a love filled with paradoxes. It makes sense inwardly. It makes no sense outwardly. Strange love is transcendental, it is rooted in friendship, otherworldly magic, and mutual care. The light burns and the shadow obscures. Love has often rendered me lonely, I've never been able to share the stories or thoughts that have weighed the most heavily upon my heart and soul.

    Sometimes strange love lies somewhere between friendship and romance. Sometimes strange love is fleeting and exists between strangers. It's unexpected, it runs deep and it changes the course of your life. I once met someone at a London history event. We become unlikely friends. He was a roadman historian and personality - honest, unusual, and very funny. At the time I was working as a shop assistant at a museum and he was working as a shop assistant at a historical palace. We lived twenty minutes away from each other, but only met once during our entire friendship. We both lived similar, yet very different lives. We were both dreamers, we were both wanting to grow our projects, we could both be ourselves around each other – our most ridiculous, stupid, and strange selves. We would speak on the phone every day for hours.

    Our friendship was an escape, a joyous escape. We had both been to the same university, round about the same time but never met. We both had alter egos, that few knew about. We never met, every time we planned to meet, he would cancel and come up with an excuse. I knew deep down that our friendship or whatever it was we were in, was becoming increasingly toxic. He was emotionally unstable and could be so difficult, but I loved him, as a friend, sometimes as something more. Eventually, our friendship made me feel bad, it made me feel empty and even more alone. I withdrew. I became tired of his empty promises and his erratic mood swings. Our lives were entirely different but there was a red string that connected us. I've left friends for much less than what he did, but for some reason, he had a hold on me. It's so rare that we meet someone with who we can be our entire selves, but often when we do there's a catch. He encouraged me to continue working hard and to never abandon my dreams. It was a strange love, and like every strange love I've experienced, it had a strange ending. Many things were left unsaid, and that's how they'll forever remain.

Parental Love

"A father's goodness is higher than the mountain, a mother's goodness deeper than the sea." — Japanese Proverb

My appreciation and love for my parents grows every time I visit Lahore. My mum and dad have been my lifelong guides. Every time I'm in Lahore, I'm reminded how much they've sacrificed, how much they've endured and how far from home they've found themselves. I wonder if they ever felt a sense of belonging, in the foreign lands in which they spent the greater part of their lives, or the motherland they no longer claim in the way they used to.

    I feel pain for my mum especially. Here she is so loved and respected and cared for by her sisters, and her nieces and nephews. Her children fell short in these respects. My cousins are so doting and selfless. They pay so much attention to their parents, they take care of them always. It brings me peace and it makes me feel a sense of heightened guilt. I have always carried it with me. I have so much love and respect for my mum. I see her in a way that I don't in London. I watch her express herself in her mother language. I watch her offer advice and watch her busy herself with chores. My mum is a businesswoman, she is a philanthropist, she is a holy woman. She is so wonderful in so many ways. I think about the loss she's faced on her own, and how her own life has been one of solitude, of things unsaid and a silent disappointment at the way some things turned out – but she always possesses a sense of optimism, wisdom and empathy and love for people and for animals.

    I see more of myself in my mum with each passing day we have spent together in Lahore – our weaknesses and sense of fractured self. My mother has loved us and devoted her life to her family – she has so many talents, she's creative and kind and someone with morals and a strong sense of self. I've always aspired to be like my mum – to be as at peace as she is. Before I left, I expressed my concern to my sister, that my mum and I, who are often at odds with one another about most things, would be spending so much time together. My sister told me to be who my mum needs me to be, my sister told me that my mum is a holy woman and I can learn so much from her. I see it now. I wish I could love like my mum in a way that is measured but healing. I wish I loved in the right ways.

I once led a Secret Garden tour for a group that consisted mostly of mothers and daughters. I remember watching the pairs wander around each garden arm in arm chatting away. I felt a joy and a curiosity. Mother and daughter relationships can be fractured and difficult, but they can also be magical, filled with warmth and mutual care.

These days I miss my dad greatly. I miss going for walks with him and hearing his stories. My dad is the best storyteller of them all. I miss hearing his jokes, and tales of his childhood adventures and I miss listening to his advice. I miss hearing him share his knowledge. I miss his love.

The love of our parents is often a selfless love. It is a love that doesn't compare to any other love. It is nurturing, it helps us to grow into the people we need to be. I pray to God that my ideas surrounding love are purified.

On Being a Woman of Colour

"I always looked upon the acts of racist exclusion, or insult, as pitiable, for the other person. I never absorbed that. I always thought that there was something deficient about such people." — Toni Morrison

I watched in admiration as a smartly dressed Pakistani man talked into his microphone. He was giving a tour of the beautiful ruins, of fading grandeur – sharing secret histories and tales to a group of somewhat bored looking art students. I didn't understand too much of what he was saying, but I felt an unspoken kinship with him.

I've always felt a kinship with other guides, especially guides I've met abroad. I remember befriending a guide in Pompeii and speaking to a guide in Hanoi. I asked so many questions about their work and what it was like being a guide in their patch of the world. The fellowship of the guides. It's a unique experience, to show, to share, to act as a mediator, and explainer, and sometimes a minder. I would feel their pain when people didn't return on time, or when someone was rude or difficult. There are many guides who inspire me. Frieda, who grew up Satmar Hasidic and is a tour guide in Brooklyn's Hasidic neighbourhood. Huda, who leads tours in Brixton sharing lesser known stories surrounding Black Women Activists and the realities of the Brixton riots. Minji, who takes groups around Chinatown, shares the history of the community and introduces people to local eateries. In particular, I'm drawn to guides who are personally connected to spaces and narratives and who enable others access to them.

My own journey towards becoming a guide, has been anything but conventional. As a youngish British Pakistani hijab-wearing woman, I've always been acutely aware of how unconventional my life choices have been within my community and outside of it. Nothing makes me feel this sense of difference more than being in Lahore. Growing up I never seemed to fit in with any group. Many Asian girls in my school were interested in things that I wasn't very interested in, like shopping and boys and Bollywood. I tried to fit in at one point; I'd attend melas where Jay Sean and Raghav, at the time diaspora idols, would play. I tried to dress conventionally, I'd try to speak like my peers, I tried to belong. But I grew tired of trying. I became more of a social recluse; I'd spend most of my break times and lunch times in the library reading books. I loved reading more than anything. I loved seeking escape through stories.

In my teens I became more interested in indie music, outsider art, exploring and watching foreign films. I sought to be someone who took an interest in almost everything. I loved to learn about different cultures and visit different spaces. I remember once, when I was sixteen, I went to Riverside Studios in Hammersmith to see a double matinee alone. I watched two black and white movies, the first was Grand Hotel, starring Great Garbo. I was the only person of colour in the theatre and under the age of fifty. I always found myself being the odd one out, in so many different ways, in so many different places and contexts and from a very young age. Sometimes I didn't mind, but other times I felt insecure.

I always dreamed of having an interesting life. It was more important to me than being rich or having a good job. I wanted to have an interesting life, like my dad who had worked hundreds of jobs, who loved exploring and who always had so many colourful stories to share from his childhood. He shared stories of walking all night through gullies, swimming in the canals, going to the pictures once in a while with his friends (one of his friend's dads was a cinema operator), doing odd jobs as a child to survive. My dad had always been the odd one out – he had always been more than extraordinary. He'd always been independent. From a very young age he attended a boarding school and madrassah (the "House of Goodness") where he developed character traits like discipline and hard work. He got a scholarship to attend high school. His friends in high school all went on to live equally extraordinary lives, one was a painter, another a stenographer, one became a chief engineer. My dad never felt a deep sense of connection to his family as he lived away from them most of his life. My dad has always been my greatest inspiration.

As children of immigrants, we are blessed in that our parents have so much life experience. Their lives have been varied, immensely rich, and strange and wondrous, filled with lessons and learnings. My dad always encouraged my sisters and I to follow our passion, to walk our paths and to explore the options that often seem endless. Maybe this is why we each found ourselves going down very different paths. Our parents instilled within us a sense of confidence, to be who we wanted to be and to belong anywhere, although it wasn't easy. It never is.

Throughout my life, I found myself to be in a minority - whether in undertaking practical conservation work with a group of burly men out on the north downs, or when following through on courses in things like stained glass and ceramics, or working a myriad of jobs, each one very different from the last.

I often found myself in situations where I'd feel ostracized and left out for being different – micro aggressions littered my life. I was often judged, overlooked or underestimated. I remember whilst working in public relations, I'd be speaking to Conservative MPs in Richmond and they would ask if I was volunteering or if I was an intern. Or while out on a site visit someone would mansplain what a grass snake was to me, despite the fact I'd worked at wetland reserves for years or I'd be asked, in a patronizing way, what my parents thought of my career. It was demoralizing and exhausting, having to constantly "explain" yourself and justify your presence in certain spaces. Sometimes I would get so tired of simply being the other that I would lose motivation. I once got fired from an unpaid internship at the London Wildlife Trust whilst seeking to change careers. I tried to explain to a colleague all the things that were problematic and made it difficult for people of colour to engage with the sector – the language, the very concept of an unpaid internship, the lack of financial prospects and security which were ever more important if you were raised in a working class family.

The more years that passed the more confident I felt in my often-scattered identity and the more I sought friendships with people who shared similar experiences to me. People who didn't quite belong, who didn't fit neatly into boxes and who were equally averse to labels and defining themselves through their work. I've always been drawn for this reason to outsiders, often people of colour because I felt they were of my kind. They were people I could be myself with, let me guard down, vent, laugh, cry with – they understood the struggle and we shared a deeper bond because of that.

Gender

"I am no bird; and no net ensnares me: I am a free human being with an independent will." — Charlotte Brontë, Jane Eyre

A few weeks before I arrived in Lahore, I found myself in Paperchase seriously contemplating whether or not to buy an emergency mustache and beard that was on sale. It would make things a lot easier for me in Lahore, I thought. I could go where I pleased and wander the streets more freely. I could even turn my experiences of pretending to be a man, into a short story, I'm sure it would be in parts tragic, hilarious and telling. I didn't end up buying it.

Sometimes I wonder how my life might have been different if I had been born a boy. It's been on my mind more and more since coming to Pakistan. Here, I am so much more aware of my identity as a woman and the limitations that my gender places upon me.

Growing up, many of my hobbies and pastimes were rather boyish (especially for an Asian girl). I enjoyed going on adventures, skateboarding, exploring, hiking – my least favourite places were shopping centres, I had no interest in fashion or make up. As I grew older, I began to love being a woman. I realised the privileges my gender afforded me (as opposed to the obstacles). I was more easily let into spaces. It was easier for me to get away with trespassing and exploring places out of limits, with my camera and curiosity and my ability to disarm people through conversation.

When I first started to embark on long walks in the UK, I wondered how safe it would be to stay in hostels and traverse empty spaces as a lone woman. After my first few hikes, it became something I seldom gave much thought to. I've always been foolhardy and don't often feel a sense of fear (perhaps to my detriment). I've embarked on wanderings (urban and wild) in areas and spaces that have been deemed unsafe for visibly Muslim women to walk alone. There have only been a few rare occasions where I've felt unsafe or especially vulnerable.

I feel a sense of frustration here in Lahore for not being able to wander freely. The last time I was here, I articulated this feeling in a poem I wrote called 'The Rapunzel of Bagbanpura." In the poem, I projected my own feelings of being trapped onto a woman who was braver and gutsier than I. The Rapunzel of Baghbanpura escaped from her tower and hitched a ride in a rickshaw. She vowed that she would never abide by any law that rendered her unfree. She spent her days wandering down Grand Trunk Road conversing with poets and pilgrims, playing cricket with street children and helping strained mules carry their heavy loads. She would pitch a tent wherever she went using her chador and some sticks. She never gave a toss about the politics of being a woman. The Rapunzel of Bagbaanpura thrived against all odds. Writing gave me an opportunity to see things differently, to entertain lighter possibilities.

Over the years, I've learnt that although the societal pressures that come with being a brown Muslim woman are great – they can also be navigated with ease if we allow ourselves the freedom to liberate ourselves – and for me mental and spiritual freedom lies at the root of all other freedoms. To be able to see things differently, to imagine different lives for yourself and what those lives could entail, to essentially believe in your abilities, in your worth – to love yourself enough to give yourself a real chance. The most important lesson I have learnt about womanhood, is the importance of listening to your own inner voice – sometimes that means distancing yourself from others - from their views and beliefs that can often cloud your own.

As a woman it is so important to surround yourself with women who lift you, who want to see you succeed and vice versa. Who don't make you feel small for going against the grain, for shunning convention and doing what you feel is best for you.

I've been blessed to have had many independent, ambitious and resilient female friends of colour. Friends who have worked so hard to actualize their dreams. These friends have constantly inspired me. I've cheered for them from the fringes as they've achieved their hard-fought for goals.

I once had a close friend; a Brazilian ecologist named Aline. She was tomboyish, persistent and daring. She pushed herself to reach her career goals, spurred on by a deep and genuine love for wildlife and the natural world. We met at the London Wetland Centre where we both worked part-time. In the weeks before I left to travel, we struck up an unlikely friendship. We realised that we had a lot more in common than we first thought. In the years that followed, we embarked on countless adventures together. We watched the sunset from Reigate Hill after circling Holmethorpe Lagoons, walked the South Downs at twilight, clambered over stone faces at Harrison Rocks, traversed a crystal grotto and a neon wonderland. I loved listening to her stories - of carrying out bat and newt surveys throughout hidden lands owned by the Ministry of Defence. I loved her adventurous spirit, her honesty, humour and openness. She encouraged me always to bravely walk the path less travelled and to be unafraid to make decisions that others may never understand.

I spent a lot of time with female friends who had very different ideas and lives to my own. Often and not purposely, they made me feel small and as though my life and way of living was incorrect, selfish and lacking. They pushed ideas like marriage and a stable career onto me, until I felt myself grow depressed and anxious. It took me a long while to realise that the people who love you, and who have been in your life for the longest time, may not know you very well and don't always know what's best for you. Self-sufficiency and self-preservation are important characteristics for development, the ability to be alone and to make your own decisions, to own your life is so valuable and necessary – to erect boundaries and to be vocal in maintaining them is key.

Womanhood is often equated with motherhood, especially in South Asia. The qualities that it's taken me a lifetime to cultivate in the West are sometimes seen to be qualities somewhat unbefitting of women in Lahore – to be vocal, to think freely, to cultivate creativity and to be open, warm and independent. I've never dreamed of a wedding, of having children, of building and anchoring myself to a home. All these things are often portrayed to be central to the lives and ambitions of a woman. They have never been central to mine. We get to define our own meaning of womanhood and what it means to be a good woman.

Being a guide has also been a saving grace for me on so many levels. Through my wanderings and community work, I've met women who are inspiring, open and kind. There are many kinds of beautiful lives, just as there are many versions of womanhood.

*

Last night my male cousins and I sat on the rooftop, we listened to music, shared jokes and laughter, took the piss out of each other. It felt like nothing had changed. I had felt like one of the boys. They were into exploring and adventuring and seeking out new frontiers. During my visit, I've become very fond of my cousin Hajji. He's seventeen, he's tough and foolhardy - he rides a motorbike, climbs on top of rooftops, dives into unknown waters, spends time with his ever-growing gang of friends. He works at his dad's restaurant till 2am every morning. I see a bit of myself in him, his grit and the way he allows himself to enjoy life but at the same time work hard. The other night, his motorbike broke down when he was returning from the restaurant. There was a rainstorm and he had to walk back with it. He told me that he loved the feeling, of being in the rain, of lugging his bike back in the early hours of the morning. It was sort of magical. I understood completely.

Guiding

"Do not go where the path may lead, go instead where there is no path and leave a trail." — Ralph Waldo Emerson

"Where are you from?" I get asked this question a lot while guiding, especially from those who aren't from the UK. It's a question that arises out of curiosity but it's a wearisome question. When you think of a tour guide in Britain, often you'd think of a blue badge guide, usually an older white middle- or upper-class man or woman.

My very identity as a guide is sometimes seen to be problematic. I don't look like a 'native.' It's hard to be accepted sometimes let alone celebrated. As a result, I have to do a lot more emotional labour, I have to go the extra mile to make others feel comfortable with my role. I've never met a woman of colour, Muslim, hijab-wearing guide. At least not in London. I'm sure and hopeful they must exist, but I imagine they are few in numbers and there are a million cultural reasons for this. How does one become a guide even? Where does one get the idea? Is there any money in it? Any prestige? Any joy?

I'd never been on a tour before I began guiding. In my early twenties, I started leading group hikes for Muslim women to places like the South Downs National Park. For me, it was a way of giving back, sharing my passion and enabling others the opportunity to get out into the countryside. It can take much confidence and courage to leave the city, especially as young Muslim women of colour. On our hikes, we sometimes encountered racism, name calling, dirty looks, unkind assertations – but we kept walking, kept laughing, kept claiming space. It wasn't an easy thing to do, to organise and lead these excursions. Often people would turn up to the station late and miss the train, I had to convince people that they would be safe. I felt responsible when things went wrong. I'd always complete recces beforehand. Sometimes the weather was awful. Once we went for a hike in the depths of winter, it was raining heavily throughout, a lot of the girls didn't have the right footware or waterproofs, there were a few falls, I was worried people might get sick. We arrived back at our starting point as the sky darkened. We felt relived and rejuvenated despite the setbacks. It was magical, it was always worth it when we as a group returned safely and were in amazing spirits. We'd take breaks to pray in a cave. We would form close connections; strangers would become close friends. We would enjoy natural beauty.

A few years prior I got involved in Mosaic, a project that sought to bring more people of colour into the UK's beautiful national parks. I undertook many workshops, from map reading in the New Forest with a park ranger to practical conservation on the Downs. My involvement in the project deepened my passion for the environment and natural spaces. I began my journey towards working in conservation, it was a wholly frustrating and difficult journey. I had job interviews with the South Downs National Park Authority and at National Trust sites outside of London. I wasn't successful. The field of work felt impenetrable. I didn't feel like they were environments I would belong in. I valued diversity and being around different kinds of people. All the while I would still embark on adventures in the edgelands, during a time of heightened Islamophobia and back when I wore my hijab in a more traditional way.

When we feel we may not be able to thrive and get ahead through conventional routes, we carve out new ways for ourselves. It's difficult, but often necessary. Innovation comes to us, I feel, when we have exhausted other avenues, when we feel the right one doesn't exist. I started to lead walks when I was unemployed. I needed a bit of cash while my savings were depleting, and I thought it would be a fun way to share my passion and make spaces accessible, especially for women of colour.

My first wandering tour was a secret Wandle walk. I shared personal stories and anecdotes and stories I'd collected whilst working on an oral history project about the River Wandle for work. I arranged for a man named John Hawke to open the remains of the Merton Priory Chapter House and give us a private talk on the mysterious space under an A road. We visited the Wheelhouse Potter, William Morris' former Liberty print works. I shared stories of an artist named Jane Porter who created an alphabet from things she found in the river, and who organised a floating lantern festival, and who made a coracle and floated down the waterway in it. I told the stories of Bob, who wrote a book about the river. I shared personal connections elders and children had formed with the river. We visited the city farm afterwards and we wandered in the wetlands. The group was mostly formed of friends and friends of friends. I felt self-conscious throughout.

I remember on that first tour, one of my friends asked why she had to pay five pounds to attend the walk. I felt embarrassed and weird. I consequently lowered the price to three pounds. The idea of a walking tour felt culturally alien to people. My mum hated the idea – she didn't feel it was Islamic to take to strangers on a walk, especially men. I enjoyed it and kept going, although it was difficult, sometimes thankless.

I received my first big break when the Londonist featured my Tooting Tour on their weekly list of things to do. I was in Copenhagen when I found out. I couldn't believe so many random people were booking on and soon discovered it was because it had been listed. I felt nervous but happy. I was very sick at the time. I had developed a very bad cough that wasn't going away, but I couldn't cancel. I led the walk, there were times I could barely breathe let alone talk. It went very well though. People were kind, except for these two women who had come all the way from Kent. They were standoffish, and left early - just before a talk I had arranged with the curator of the Sewing Machine Museum. I tried not to let it bother me, everyone else was nice enough and I'd actually made a few solid connections.

At the end of the walk, a group of us went to Chennai Dosa for lunch. It was a lovely diverse group. We ate together, laughed and talked. An elderly English lady ordered a spicy dosa and enjoyed it so much. Two years on she left a review on TripAdvisor expressing how much she enjoyed the day and how happy she felt afterward. Many of the attendees came to the next wandering, and so marked the beginning of my renegade guiding career. You learn lessons as you go. You learn to let go of negativity - to be positive and to give attention to those who are receptive and open.

Although I have experienced many challenges that have left me feeling hopeless and sad, my positive experiences have been far greater and more memorable. Over the years, I've learnt not to care so much about how people perceive me. I've developed the courage to be disliked. I do my best, and leave the rest to God. Vulnerability is a superpower - by being your authentic self, you allow for others to be themselves too. Not everyone will like you or accept you and that's okay. For me, the most important thing is to keep my tours and events as open and accessible as possible, so no one feels left out or out of place.

Business

"In the midst of chaos, there is also opportunity" — Sun-Tzu

When it comes to business, I have always struggled. As a woman of colour with no professional guiding qualifications, asking for money has always been difficult. The journey from charging nothing to charging something, has been reflective of my fluctuating self-esteem. Over the years I've increased in confidence and have learnt to value what I do to a much greater degree.

Having nothing to go by, I have been forced to innovate, to generate new ideas, to think up new clients and ways of doing things in an ever-evolving world. When I first started to have meetings with hotel managers, I felt out of my depth. I was asking for money to create events and tours, something that had not been done before. I had to clearly explain the value of what I was offering. I was sometimes met with curiosity, sometimes incredulity 'You want us to pay you, to run an event in our space?!'

It took persistence, creativity, grit and a lot of self-belief. I remember once I had a meeting with a Cultural Engineer named Tas from Ace Hotel. It took me a very long time to convince him to commission me to run tours and workshops and to additionally create content for Ace Reader, the brand's online lifestyle magazine. I remember at one point in the meeting, I crossed out an initial price and told him I was happy to do the work for less. In response, he gave me a number that was much greater. I left feeling valued. As a Muslim woman, I'm aware I live in a culture where my kind are constantly disparaged, put down and made to feel lesser, these ideas seep into the recesses of our psyches, causing damage that takes a long time to counter.

It took me a very long time to see the value in what I did, it took much reassurance and many big breaks for me to finally charge what I needed to live. I felt I didn't belong in the spaces in which I was pitching my ideas, slick hipster hotels and bourgeois educational institutes. I had imposter syndrome for the longest time. I kept thinking of all that I lacked – business acumen, in depth historical knowledge, a clue! What was I doing in these places? Sometimes I felt like a beggar. Sometimes I felt like I was on the top of my game. Business was filled with setbacks, highs and lows – everything felt personal.

What I did have was ten years' worth of insider information, countless stories of amazing London people and places, and that was invaluable. You couldn't find those stories of spaces in books, you found them through exploring, making connections, learning, and putting forward your learnings. My business was borne out of curiosity, passion, and a desire to connect people, to share what I felt to be valuable and to encourage people to walk the road less travelled. In every business meeting, I sought always to be authentic, honest and to express my intentions as fully as possible. I learnt to adapt, to seek out collaborations, to identify who I wanted to work for and what projects most interested me. To own your own knowledge, for it to be unique and meaningful, it feels more valuable than gaining a badge, a certificate or any qualification. I'm beginning to understand that now.

Power and Solidarity

"The most common way people give up their power is by thinking they don't have any." — Alice Walker

Despite all the challenges that come with being a woman of colour guide, there is also tremendous power in it, especially in a city as diverse and multilayered as London. You're able to connect with communities more authentically, to guide them, to speak a language they understand – your language. You possess a compassion and duality that is difficult to understand and enact if you have never been the *other*. I feel like the commissions I receive are more interesting, relevant, and varied than that of other guides and that's something I truly appreciate. Often it's the community walks I'm commissioned to do, especially for elders, that are the most fun and engaging.

When leading walks for a mostly middle-class white audience, I notice that I speak a bit posher and stand a bit taller. I no longer admonish myself for this - to be adaptable and relate to people where they are is part of my job, but to do so in an authentic way is so important. I hate the idea of being put in a box and have never tried to make a name for myself as the first female British Muslim Pakistani guide in London. I find the narrative trite and boring.

I used to organise bi-monthly Citizens of London talks on behalf of citizenM hotels. My role was to find and interview inspiring Londoners about their life journey, to find out about their worlds. I would always choose other renegades, mostly renegades of colour, whose stories inspired me greatly. I interviewed people I sought in one way or another to emulate. I interviewed Saad Eddine Said, a Moroccan Creative Director who created projects rooted in art and activism. Chanmi had met him in Busan. He was in London leading a city take over at Battersea Arts Centre. I interviewed him about his journey. I asked whether art could create lasting change and understanding between communities. We spoke about the value of political activism across borders. I interviewed a former boss, Kemi Akinola, the director of Brixton People Kitchen and founder of the community canteens. Kemi spent years providing space and meals for those in need. She shared stories of helping out in a soup kitchen in Skid Row in LA. She talked about her extraordinary personal journey into food and community work following a car accident which left her in a coma. I interviewed Rachel Wang, founder of Chocolate Films, a film director and businesswoman, a leader in the heritage field. She initiated the '1,000 Londoners' film project featuring the stories of diverse and interesting Londoners. I interviewed the Urban Birder, David Lindo – a broadcaster, birder and author. I interviewed Jay Richards, the charismatic CEO of an organization that sought to provide at risk young people the opportunity to start their own businesses.

   I was grateful for the opportunity to provide inspiring individuals with a platform to share their unique stories, challenges and insights. They were people I could personally relate to, people who inspired me with their work and more importantly, their character. Their stories gave me permission to take greater risks – to find peace and meaning through work. Kindness begets kindness and I am always grateful for the people I've met in my life who have encouraged me to keep going. I feel especially inspired by humble people who work for their own communities and who do not seek validation or glory for the lives they live and the choices they make. People who do what they do out of joy and an inner need. Everyday people on my Instagram timeline - who don't have a great deal of followers - everything they post is authentic, honest, real: a young lady who cycles across the African continent alone, a young man who takes people on excursions to the mountains. I've met hundreds of people like this on my journey – unlikely kindred spirits. I met K - a female filmmaker who started up a film production company and made horror films: Maya and Black Lake. Black Lake was partly set in a Necropolis in Pakistan. She self-funded it and, at the end, screened it at the Prince Charles Cinema for friends, family and supporters. I met Virginia, an artist and community activist who spent years managing environmental regeneration initiatives across London and now works mainly with food.

I love to share the stories of unsung renegades on my wandering tours too. I was commissioned to create a tour sharing the stories of inspiring female Londoners for the Museum of London. The walk was called In Her Footprints, and it focused on real life stories of incredible selfless women of colour who remained largely unknown - foster mums, carers, community leaders, elderly activists, cooks, artists, writers – wondrous women from all walks of life. In film and literature, I've similarly been drawn to stories of people of colour, stories of people's connections to space and passion for expression, stories of people like Rodriguez from Searching for Sugarman', and Jimmy from 'The Last Black Man of San Francisco'. Someone once told me the thing that makes you different is the very thing that gives you your edge, and that it is important to walk into your weakness – to claim it and turn it into your power. I went from being an "unqualified" novice tour guide to becoming a "renegade" guide. My change in perception, and the way I used language to redefine myself and my vocation, set me free.

*

In Lahore, the days seem longer, and I have much more time to think. I've been daydreaming a lot recently about setting up a tour company in my motherland, but as a woman, the challenges of doing so feel immense and the rules of society feel unbreakable. Yet I wonder if maybe that's just the bubble I'm in. The other day I went to Bahria Town with my cousins and my mum. Bahria Town is a new shiny town on the outskirts of the city. It's home to art installations, green spaces, a beautiful mosque and a small Eiffel Tower. The roads are clean, and it feels like you're in a western country. It's quiet and safe.

My mum suggested we buy a place in Bahria Town and live there. It's far from the centre, but it lacks the soul and character of the places in Lahore I've become familiar with. To live in and among the people is something I've always felt strongly about. My cousins don't like Bahria Town very much, they miss the "shor and sharaba" noise and madness of the neighbourhood they live in. Neighbourhoods aren't easy, from my experiences, to live in, least not in the way I'm used to living. Deep down, I know that I'll struggle in find a lasting home in Lahore, however much I want too, and however much my mum wants too. My mum said to me the other day, "Say what you want, this is my land, my country – however flawed and difficult it may be, it is my home".

It is a beautiful country and I would love, one day, to share with others its beauty through excursions, through leading tours or opening a hotel. It feels like a pipe dream, but it will always be there, in the back of my mind - a possibility, a new life.

On Community

"In every community, there is work to be done. In every nation, there are wounds to heal. In every heart, there is the power to do it." — Marianne Williamson

London is home to so many diverse, unique and inspirational communities. Over the years, I've worked with many of them on various oral history, heritage, food, environmental and creative projects. I've organised and been involved in many events that seek to bring people together, celebrate cultures and draw light upon stories.

I've worked with groups of Nepalese, Irish, Somali, Pakistani and Caribbean elders. I've led wanderings for various community groups – photographers, writers, young entrepreneurs, as well as for hotel staff and guests. I've led workshops for women's groups. I've led wanderings for groups of businessmen and businesswomen. I've helped organise skate offs, undertaken community consultations in housing estates across London. I've filmed talent shows, and community garden openings. I've photographed primary school assemblies on air pollution. I've watched elders knit scarves for kittens at the animal rescue centre in Tottenham. I've met with craftspeople who upcycle furniture at Western Riverside Waste Authority. I've attended resident association meetings and sports grounds opening. I remember at one event, Jeremy Corbyn sat next to me and asked me how things were. We enjoyed a chat and a slice of cake together.

The first job I ever had was at a pharmacy in Clapham. I worked there part-time for over three and a half years. I loved my job. I loved the people that came in. I'd often talk to the regulars. I learnt a lot from the elders, those recovering from drug addiction, those terminally ill and those getting better. I've always sought ways to combine my love for community work with my love for creativity and the environment. Working as a Communications Officer for an environmental regeneration charity was perfect as the job focused as much on people as places. For a while it was my dream job – I loved travelling across London, sharing stories of incredible people, accessing spaces and having a stable income. Quitting my job to work on Living London, to undertake freelance projects and, ultimately, to travel was one of the most difficult decisions I ever made. Since then, I've got into a cycle of getting a job (often in the arts, heritage or social work sectors), working on my own projects on the side, then quitting the job, and growing my projects on the side. Being a freelancer and the owner of a small business is exhausting, but immensely rewarding.

My work is varied and often self-initiated. As well as leading wandering tours in different areas across the city, I also run workshops through which I teach people how to create their own walking tours connecting spaces that are meaningful and interesting to them. I receive a myriad of special commissions from diverse clients including hotels, community groups, charities and local authorities. Examples of such commissions range from creating and leading explorative memory tours for elders and running storytelling workshops for young people, to creating and delivering themed micro-tours aimed at encouraging local people to use cleaner air walking routes. Often the lines between being a community worker and a renegade guide blur, both are about people and place – and strengthening the ties between them. There's so much synchronicity in my line of work. I often meet people again and again, in unlikely places.

I once led a private tour for two lovely Spanish women, we happened to have attended the same university and we had so much in common. Whilst wandering through Abney Park Cemetery, which itself has over the years become a magnet for otherworldly encounters, we bumped into a mysterious lady named Shannon, someone I knew but would come to know a lot better in the months that followed. My day job then involved co-managing three community canteens alongside a chef/friend, Jess. The canteens were open to the public, anyone was welcome to come along and enjoy a free healthy delicious vegetarian meal made wholly of surplus food. It provided a safe social space mostly for vulnerable people.

Every Monday morning Jess and I would meet at the car park at the back to Borough Market where we would pile throwaway fruit and veg into our trolleys and drag them onto a bus to the United Reform church. We held our Castle Canteen out of the church. Of the three canteens, Castle was my favourite. We were able to build a community. I got to know everyone who came, I became familiar with their characters and stories. We came to be a family – albeit a very strange and dysfunctional family. The canteen attracted misfits of all ages and backgrounds. People would share the most interesting conversations about conspiracy theories, the welfare state, western music, old films, alien abductions. Love affairs blossomed and perished. It felt like a TV show. It reflected a South London that was fast fading, located close by to East Street Market and the demolished Heygate Estate. Many of those who attended had lived in the area their whole lives. Slowly they were being pushed out. They felt it.

I met Shannon at the Castle Canteen. She would come in sometimes. She was a young and intelligent Irish woman, a therapist who had been through a lot in her life. We became unlikely friends. She was especially interested in the memory tours I was working on at the time. I had been commissioned to create a tour that shared the stories of, and highlighted the shared history and experiences of, Irish and Pakistani migrants who arrived in North London in the fifties and sixties. Shannon was adopted. Her birth parents had met in Kilburn. Her brother was a Sufi. She attended the tour –

we visited a Sufi Mosque, and the Pakistani Community Centre where Nusrat Fateh Ali Khan performed. I shared stories and insights I had collated, of music and poetry, tradition and religion, family, politics and racial profiling. I shared the stories of those I'd interviewed, the selfless Pakistani community workers and Irish builders and nurses.

We stopped off at the Galtymore and The Crown Pub and Cricklewood bus garage, the place where members of the two communities interacted. In the bus garage, we visited the control room and the locker room, there were Irish clover stickers on the fronts of some. We went to the games room where young Jamaicans were playing snooker. The tour ended at Gladstone Park; another neutral space shared by the two communities. Other attendees of the walk included local history buffs, a councillor and another canteen buddy named Bob, an older white man who wore colourful Ghanaian prints and was a mathematician and musician. A lonely man. At the end of the walk, we went for tea together.

The tour was commissioned by the Heritage Lottery Fund as part of the Generations of Learning project with Ashford Place, a charity that delivers support to disadvantaged and marginalised people. It was one of my favourite projects. It gave me an opportunity to learn about my roots and to connect with the experiences and narratives of Pakistanis of my parents' generations. As part of my work, I got to meet, know and become part of (for a very brief time) a community of Pakistani women. It was also the first time I was able to involve my mum in my work and explain to her fully what I did. We listened to oral histories together. I think my mum was moved by it. My mum never liked my line of work, but she let me be.

The local councillor, Tariq Darr, invited my mum and I to a feast taking place at the Pakistani Community Centre in Cricklewood. The women would all be there. I convinced my mum to attend with me. She gave in and we went together. Once we arrived, I introduced her to everyone, including my favourite Pakistani Auntie, Auntie Razia. She had previously shared with me the story of her life. Soon after she lost her parents, she followed her husband to England, where he was working as an engineer. Ten years ago he unexpectedly passed away and a few years ago she tragically lost her beloved son, who was aged only twenty-five, in a car accident. Despite her loss, Auntie Razia radiated warmth, positivity and faith, as did everyone at the centre. Other aunties were foster carers or teachers, or housewives. Before engaging in the project, my experiences of the Pakistani community were largely negative. I found people to be small minded, hurtful and superficial, concerned only with marriage and offspring and wealth. The women at the centre were different. They taught me humility, kindness and the importance of self-respect. My mother and I left the lunch feeling incredibly grateful and connected.

I once met a group of Nepalese women who I came to admire greatly. I'd been assigned to visit Bostall Gardens in Plumstead to take photographs. The Mayor of Greenwich was due to make an appearance. As part of a Cultivating Communities project, migrant growers had transformed a wasteland into a thriving green space. When I arrived in the garden, I was met with a group of women dressed in beautiful colourful saris and fabrics, with beautiful weathered faces, digging and planting and laughing together. In the background stood a glorious polytunnel. I felt as though I'd stepped into a different country. As I floated, I overheard a few words that I recognized. Some of the Nepalese women spoke Hindi. I could communicate with them.

I spoke to a woman wearing a baseball cap with a weed leaf sewn on, she had a strong face, charisma and brilliant sense of humour. Her name was Toku. I was drawn to her, and so were all her friends. She called me bhaji (sister) and told me of how gardening was a nice way to pass time, and how she was living alone in England, she was a widow. She told me that Bostall Gardens reminded her of home, it gave her the chance to spend time with her friends. I was inspired by her. I wanted to learn more. We talked and talked and she told me to stay away from 'baadmashes' (gangsters) who take drugs and she told me real men are hard to find. I felt privileged to be able to communicate with them. I felt like I understood these women, more than that, I felt like they understood me - the dualism of my life, and my home. Following the visit, and having received wonderful feedback for the photos and the rapport I had developed in a short time, I was commissioned to work on a film project, documenting their stories of home through song and craft. It was a long and beautiful project, at the end of which, the film was screened in Woolwich Community Centre in front of the elders, their friends and families.

Sometimes we find belonging, warmth and acceptance with other communities. It is a privilege to be able to learn from and experience another culture firsthand. Curiosity is often met with enthusiasm. I once worked at a Somali charity. In my first week, I found myself at a conference, I was the only person out of eight hundred who wasn't Somali. The women embraced me, were kind and welcoming. I learnt about their language. I learnt about Somali politics, geography, culture. I drank shaah hawash tea, got to wear a beautiful dirac, and to go to Somali restaurants. I watched them dance. I developed very close relationships with my colleagues, who became friends, some soulmates. I was aware of my position as an outsider, but they never let me feel it. I've always had very close Somali friends, getting to meet their mothers, aunts, friends and cousins, deepened our understanding and appreciation of each other.

One of my closest friends, Fatuma, is an incredibly warm knowledgeable and talented writer and audio producer. Although we didn't know each in our younger years, we grew up living almost parallel lives, we listened to the same indie and rock music and watched the same TV shows and shared similar experiences of being an 'other' in the groups and environments we found ourselves in. Another of my best friends, Amel, was always keen on Japanese anime, film and fantasy. She worked in IT and had the best sense of humour and strong sense of self. Once when we were watching a film at an empty picture house theater, she went off to pray in the middle of it. I felt proud of how secure she always was with her faith - how it grounded her, and how she put her relationship with God before all else.

Another close friend, Samra, a beautiful writer, humanitarian and lover of life, always sought to self-improve and to stay active in the community. From park runs in Japan, to a half marathon in Morocco, she constantly pushed herself. Everything she did was rooted in kindness and love - a kindness and love that had emerged from pain. I love the Somali community- the poets and dreamers, the academics, the community workers, those who sought to rebuild their motherland. I longed to visit Mogadishu, to see Lido beach. Somalia, in my mind's eye was now a place of immense beauty and possibility.

I've been a stranger and a friend among many communities. It takes so much time and energy and dedication, to build trust in a community setting. I once worked as a Team Leader at an Age Activity Centre, which initially started out at the Black Elders Project. The community bought their own centre by fundraising and putting their money together decades earlier. Back then they would go on cruises to places like Cuba and Barbados. The centre was still mostly attended by Caribbean elders. It was a warm safe space, somewhere elders could come to learn new skills, to have fun, to stay active and to socialize. It was a very difficult job, dealing with safeguarding issues, managing a kitchen, working with contractors – watching the decline of older friends. I got to know the members well during my time at the centre. I got to know the choir mistress, the elderly volunteers, each had their own style, their own personalities. I got to know about their life stories and their struggles, I got to see them laugh and joke and enjoy the everyday. Some of the elders were so hilarious. I never laughed so much in any place I ever tarried. They were brutally honest, but endearing. I sometimes joined them in Tai Chi or arts and crafts. I learnt so much about West Indian culture. The way they took care of each other and expressed themselves through faith and song inspired me deeply.

    I loved organizing activities like reggae tea dances – the chef and my close friend Linda and I would join in with the dancing. We were unselfconscious and we had so much fun. Many of the elders were from different backgrounds – White, Indian, East Asian – but they all got on. Some dressed like they were attending prom, with full make up and beautiful attire. Being around elders taught me so many lessons, before taking on the job I was so scared of getting old. They taught me it's a joy, and the older we get often the better we become, in some ways we revert to our childlike ways and that in itself is so precious. I learnt from their mistakes and their hardships, from their stories. I learnt about love, and service and loneliness. I learnt about endings and being present and appreciating every day. It was a privilege to work at the centre. Intergenerational friendships are so renewing and restorative, they teach you lessons early on. I was the youngest person who had worked my role, and I felt grateful that they eventually accepted me. It broke my heart when I left and when I had to say goodbye to the elders.

Being a community worker is hard, staying is hard and leaving is harder. When I left, I was in a really dark place mentally, many things had fallen apart - another relationship, another dream. I felt like I had let everyone down. I told one of the volunteers and long-standing members that I had decided to leave, she was the matriarch of the centre. She cried. I told her I didn't feel like I belonged with the staff, she exclaimed "But you belong with us!" I'd never felt so sad and at the same time so happy. I vowed to stay connected. I attended funerals and met with the older volunteers. It wasn't the same. I found it very difficult to leave the canteen as well. Often, vulnerable people live fragile lives, they're used to being abandoned and disappointed and it affects them in deep ways when someone they come to know and trust, leaves.

I was once sitting in a walled English garden when a man wearing a top hat approached me. I recognized him as a regular from the Battersea Canteen. He took a seat next to me and began talking. He talked and talked as though he hadn't talked to anyone for the longest time. He talked about conspiracy theories, his abusive wife who he was sure used him to gain British citizenship, the scars the marriage had left him with. He talked about his failing writing career. I listened and nodded and listened and nodded. I was very tired that day, physically, mentally and existentially – I was in desperate need of quiet. After a while, I couldn't bear to listen anymore. I made something up about needing to be somewhere. He seemed a little crestfallen. We said our goodbyes. I rushed off in search of quiet empty space. I took a nap on the hill. I found him in the park a little later. I felt a crushing sense of guilt. How do you say, no it's enough - please, no more?

The guilt never leaves you. The guilt of not being able to visit old Ella at her house, to cook for her, the guilt of not being able to lend a struggling deaf man another tenner. When an elderly lady asks you to accompany her to the toilet. When a lonely man makes a pass at you. When the same people tell you the same sad stories again and again, and when you see them unravel and decline so clearly in front of you. The professional boundaries erected in order to protects us and others, often break us - they eat away at our conscience. In the past, colleagues have told me I'll find certain aspects of community roles difficult, as I have a soft heart and won't easily be able to make right decisions. It was true. There's another guilt you become familiar with too, that of privilege - of the love you receive and security you possess. It's a guilt laced with anger at the injustices that become so apparent when you see them in front of you - people are hungry, people are lonely, people are in need. You have to have a steely sense of self to be a community worker. Often, your mental health is affected. Often, it hits you like a ton of bricks. We are all unutterably alone.

As well as dealing with stress and guilt of work, I've also always seemed to develop friendships and relationships with those grappling with immense and heartbreaking problems that contribute to mental health issues. It took me a very long time to understand that I was allowed to be happy. That I didn't have to be sad always, because the people around me were. And what they needed most, was to see someone embody joy, peace and stability.

I carry with me memories, of the women I worked with at the refugee centre, the children I played with while working as a play worker, the sick elders who would come into the pharmacy. All these jobs taught me gratitude and gave me perspective. People live such different lives, they toil and they struggle and sometimes all we can really do is love them and to voice the beauty we see in them, kind sentiments we often fail to express. Words can build people, as they can tear them apart. Communities teach me about courage, togetherness and friendship. I always leave, with feelings of heightened solitude and painful gratification.

When it comes to wandering tours, my favourite commissions often involve working with community groups. The places we visit often have strong community connections, walks are more interactive, they're lighter, more fun and wholly inclusive. I once led a walk in North London aimed at older people that sought to connect them to space and each other through sharing memories of sports and activities. One attendee, an Indian woman named Kala, was very charismatic and interesting. She was a lifelong freedom fighter and women's rights activist. Her friend was much older, she had a fantastic sense of humour. We had tea together at the end, they shared bits of their life stories. The lives of older immigrants are often so layered and interesting. Almost six months later, I met Kala at another walk I was leading, this time in Erith. The walk included a trip down the longest pier in London, where I shared tales of whale watching. The wind blew and it didn't feel like London at all. We also visited a beautiful church, whereby we met members of the congregation. We visited a community hall, at the time elders inside were knitting. Every wandering tour offers opportunities to connect with a multitude of other communities.

You can find a sense of belonging and community is everyday spaces – the park, the market, the swimming pool. I once joined a women's gym in Stoke Newington, it was called Sunstone. It was a beautiful warm space. It was about an hour and a half from where I lived but I didn't mind the journey, because I loved the gym. The community was home too. In the daytime it was mostly frequented by middle-aged Jewish women and Turkish women. I'd listen in the sauna or by the poolside as they shared conversations among themselves about their husbands and in laws and religious holidays. It was a privilege to have a glimpse into lives so different, and communities, quite insular and private. My work is a lot of things, but never boring. I'm grateful for all the stories, encounters and interactions, connected and brought into being by the divine. I believe that our work should heal others, and in some small way, heal the world. With everything I do, I aim to inspire people to seek relief and wonderment in the magical every day - it's our connection to ourselves, other people and places, that often makes life worth living. These connections make us feel less alone. They instill within us a sense of togetherness, a sense of shared humanity.

On Mental Health

"Truly, it is in the darkness that one finds the light, so when we are in sorrow, then this light is nearest of all to us." — Miester Eckhart

I didn't sleep at all last night, my thoughts were so noisy and troubling, set alight by the things my aunt had said earlier on in the day, about time passing by and how I need now more than ever to settle down. I felt so unwell after she left. I lay on the mungee in my room - a sadness washed over me. Sometimes, the only thing worse than things changing is things staying the same. There was a truth in much of what she said, and I had to believe she said it out of love and care, but that didn't stop my thoughts racing, it didn't stop me from feeling panicked and unable to breathe.

Eight years ago, I dreamt that I would one day return to Lahore, and settle down in the city forever. It was a dream I never shared with anyone, because I didn't know anyone who would understand it, let alone accept and celebrate it. We live in a world where small-mindedness is widespread, people judge, but they do not seek to truly understand. Life passes by and we become so entrenched in our ways of seeing and living until one day we realize that although we have not quite outgrown our dreams, we have moved beyond them. Have I moved beyond my faded dream? Sometimes, we are given the opportunity to grab hold of everything we ever wanted – and still, we hesitate.

I've battled bouts of anxiety and depression throughout my life. These have often been triggered by difficult, sometimes incomprehensible events and experiences. When I was working at the Dino Shop at the Natural History Museum, I had a breakdown. It took me a very long time to recover. I couldn't explain it. It was at a time in my life when everything was falling apart. I was dealing with the fallout of bad decisions, immense setbacks, ill-health, and a myriad of other stresses. At the same time, I was working in a museum where I was constantly surrounded by thousands of people, noise, and movement. I reached a point where I could no longer deal. I had a breakdown. I could barely formulate sentences. I could barely function on a day to day basis. I self-medicated. I withdrew entirely.

It's during times of crisis, you discover who and what really matters. It took a long while to remove myself from that dark place. I sought refuge for a short while in Neptune Marina in Ipswich where my brother was living. It was winter. It was dark and cold and everything felt impossible. I would watch the boats at midnight. I would cry alone, often. I went back to London. I went back to work. People didn't understand. They mistook my anxiety and withdrawal for arrogance and indifference. I couldn't explain. I didn't have the energy and I didn't know how to.

I found relief in small things. In conversations shared with Dippy the diplodocus and the Blue Whale. In writing poems about the birds in the bird gallery, they spoke to me - the albatross and the parrot and the dodo, they gave me advice and voiced encouragement. They told me to keep going. I shared my problems with the giant mammoth. I sat in the Japanese supermarket while the simulated earthquake caused everything to shake and fall around me. I looked to the cosmos, to the moon. I studied gems and minerals. I would delve into a dark place whilst traversing the never-ending tunnel below the museum. My imagination made the everyday more bearable.

There were times in my life during which I found myself almost paralyzed by sickness, mental and physical, so much so that wandering became almost impossible. I would find it difficult to leave my room. Going for walks, I'd experience palpitations. I'd feel dizzy and as though I was dying. My legs felt unsteady, metres felt like miles. I felt so lonely. I pushed on. Some days, getting a train to some far-off place like Whitstable felt like the greatest achievement in the world. It snowed when I got to the sea. A passing Scotsman said hello. He said that if he were English he wouldn't have greeted me. He said most people around there were racist. We chatted for a brief while; about oysters, about the weather, about the sea. I asked if I could take his photograph. He obliged. I thanked him. We went our separate ways. It was freezing cold. I settled by the empty shore. I sipped tea. I'd prepared a thermos. My sight went blurry and I felt unsteady and I went home. I felt like I was being punished. The worse my anxiety got, the more I pushed myself – to face fears. I became reckless and angry. I would walk because I wanted to prove to myself that I wouldn't die. I would walk and walk and walk. I sought refuge in wandering, even when wandering was the most difficult thing in the world to do.

During low points in my life, whilst working jobs I struggled with, or when relationships had turned sour or my physical health had declined, I found that exploring, wandering, observing, saved me and provided me with relief and consolation. During times when I felt most abandoned, the streets were always there for me. I'd go for a wander. I'd know life would be better. I would see things and people.

Once when I felt heartbroken, I decided to go for a walk along the Southbank. I followed a blind couple for a mile. I watched as they laughed and walked slowly and experienced their surroundings. It took me out of my head, to someplace magical and beautiful. Observing affords us great power. My mental and physical health struggles, often rooted in a spiritual malaise, have, at times, chiseled away at my sanity and rendered life almost unbearable. But they have also taught me important lessons, they've taught me gratitude and resilience. I've learnt how fragile life is and how fragile we are. I've learnt to appreciate every moment.

It was during my darkest times I came to understand the value of healing and of being healed through kindness. In times of crisis, to look outside of yourself, and to seek to improve the condition of others, provides a great sense of consolation. My faith taught me a smile is charity, and so I learned to smile – and I found people would smile back, and it would be a small healing. By encouraging and praising others, by freely expressing kind sentiments in a world that is so in need of kind sentiments, is no small feat. I have always tried where I can engage in small acts of kindness, to open people up to the beauty that is within them - to me, these small acts give my life purpose. The alchemy of life is to resist allowing the suffering we feel to make us bitter, but rather to make us better – kinder and softer. Small acts of kindness are a saving grace. We all make mistakes, we cause unimaginable hurt, we perpetuate storms, carve craters in hearts and scars in souls, but we also possess the capacity to make things right again – through kindness. Sometimes, we realise that the person most in need of our kindness, is ourselves.

I worked as a gallery assistant at the Victoria and Albert Museum for a time. In between giving directions, telling people where the loo was and staring aimlessly into space, I thought a lot. I thought so much, sometimes my thoughts drove me crazy. It's a horrible feeling, to think and think and think, but to be unable to organise your thoughts or make sense of them. I was always grateful when someone spoke to me, and pulled me out of a daze. Or when someone walked by who was especially interesting or fabulous – dressed in traditional attire, a colourful sari, Japanese robes, a vintage dress. I'd let my imagination run wild.

Being a guide can be very mentally challenging. It is a performative job, it forces you to get out of yourself, to be articulate and present. There have been times when I have been completely broken, my whole life has been up in flames and my mind, a complete mess, but I've had to show up, to put on a mask, to be positive and engaging. Other times, guiding has acted as a form of escapism. I'll stretch a wandering tour out if the group is keen to keep going and if I have nothing else to do or nowhere else to go. It makes it easy to forget, for a while, about your real-life problems and all that you lack. You can be the best version of yourself, for a fleeting while, you can feel whole.

It's hard to be anonymous. I bump into people everywhere I go - at museums, in shops, on the streets, in unlikely spaces. Old friends, former colleagues, those who have come along to one of my events or tours. Sometimes I feel like a ghost in a haunted city – trying so hard to transcend, to not reenact the same scenes in the same places again and again. Sometimes I wish I could erase my memories – experience places for the first time again, and let go of difficult triggering associations.

It is also a very demanding profession, especially when leading group visits for students in cities outside of London. I remember on one occasion I lost a student at Christ Church. I searched frantically for her around Oxford city centre, only to find her enjoying lunch in an arcade cafe. I was more relieved than annoyed. I joined her for lunch. She was a painter, a fabulously talented young painter from Ukraine. She showed me her work and shared with me her aspirations. We spent most of the day together, wandering around galleries and speaking about our work. At the end of every trip, I get this sinking feeling, that maybe I counted wrong and that I had left a student behind. On another occasion, I was forced to give an impromptu tour of Westminster Abbey. I was told there would be an official guide waiting for us outside the entrance but there wasn't. I'd never been to the Abbey before and knew nothing of its history. I read off a Wikipedia page on my phone. It was embarrassing, almost comical – another one for the 'Bad Guide' chronicles, I noted in my mind.

Being a guide is stressful. It's stressful when someone doesn't understand what you're saying or when someone really needs the loo but there isn't one for miles. It's stressful when people show up late or early - when they make assumptions, unkind ones, and when they ask really difficult questions. It's stressful to always make yourself be heard, especially as an introvert. It's stressful having to talk when all you want is to stay quiet. When you no longer want to share a story because it's no longer for you - because you don't own it. It's stressful when there's a downpour or a blizzard or a storm and you have to keep going. It's stressful when you're leading a tour while you're unwell. It's stressful having to do everything yourself all the time, and to do it with a smile. It's stressful when you put so much work into a tour and only one or two people turn up. It's stressful asking for money at the end of a tour when someone hasn't paid you and there's an awkward silence. It's stressful to be direct and confident when you're feeling insecure, antisocial and depressed. Those days, I find it the hardest to be a guide. You have to put things behind you and show up no matter where you are mentally, no matter how unmotivated or uninspired you are feeling. You have to overlook the judgements of others.

I've learnt not to allow my self-worth to be greatly affected by reviews and criticisms (online and offline). I've developed the courage to be wrong, to be disliked, and to be thought little of. Being a guide makes you resilient and stoic. It makes you patient and compassionate. I try to stay positive- to ask for miracles and to believe they can come true. To ask for guidance from God. I've arrived at a point where I care much less about what people think of me. I've learned to function and thrive in the face of criticism and to try, as hard as I can, to preserve my mental health.

*

My time in Lahore is coming to an end. These days, I have found myself in a dark place, grappling desperately for meaning, clarity and faith. Physically weak and emotionally overcome, I've been spending endless stretches of time staring at the ceiling in my room thinking of all the things that have gone wrong in my life, all the mistakes I've made and the hurt I've caused. It is these cyclical feelings that have often, in the past, propelled me into the murkiest depths of depression. I wish I could go for a walk, escape from the confines of these four walls which seem to be closing in on me. It has long been my remedy for ill feelings, to walk and walk and walk, until I grow so tired that I forgot myself, and all thoughts escape me and an internal quietude reigns.

I'm trying hard to be patient – soon I will be free again, perhaps. I'm trying hard to remember that it is always darkest before the dawn, that often, during times of crisis, when nothing feels real, when your dreams fall apart – that is when we're closest to an inner revolution. It is in our suffering, in our most unshakeable feelings of despair and futility that we often draw closest to the truth, that we find the courage within us to hope and pray, that by some miracle, we will rise.

On Privilege

"When we give cheerfully and accept gratefully, everyone is blessed." — Maya Angelou

Being a renegade guide isn't easy, but it's a worthy vocation and one that I hope to never give up on. It's a privilege to be able to show people around the city I love – a city that has long been a friend to me. It's a privilege to be part of someone else's life, albeit for a fleeting while. London can be a lonely and overwhelming city for a stranger or a traveler, and it is a privilege to be able to make one's journey easier – whether that's by showing someone how to top up their Oyster card and navigate public transport, or by listening to someone speak about their dreams, hopes, and fears. It's a privilege bringing people together and watching them connect and form friendships. It's a privilege to break bread with people from different corners of the world. To enable, in some small way, others to feel a sense of belonging, a sense of possibility and hope – to me, this is what it means to be a guide. I have learnt and continue to learn so much about different cultures, creeds, and ideologies – it is humbling and inspiring.

It's a privilege to have the favour returned by so many people in so many places. On one occasion, after a book lovers tour, one of my guests, a young lady who worked at Sothesby's, took me to visit the beautiful libraries of the Oxford and Cambridge Club. It was an opulent space that had a dress code. I wasn't quite sure how I got in. But it was incredible to be shown around, to glimpse into a world so far from my own. In the ladies powder room, Japanese women were applying make-up, in the reading room, old men in suits were reading newspapers. Once an artist invited me to her studio on Eel Pie Island, a strange and colourful Island in the middle of the Thames, filled with quirky spaces and an artist's community. It used to be the home to the biggest hippie commune in the UK. A hotelier at Andaz led me to see a hidden temple that had been excavated, he switched the lights on and shared stories of the people who had used the space, people like Lady Gaga.

I've knocked on so many doors, and so often, people have let me into their spaces. A site manager allows me to explore deserted and haunted Tobacco Dock alone. A lady who looks after a Tin Tabernacle, the sea cadets' home in Kilburn, shares with me the history of the space and the stories that render it enlivened. A priest opens a church for me. A monk shows me around a temple. A friend gives me a tour of her former workplace, Chelsea Physic Garden, and introduces me to all the characters that make the space special. Another friend takes me to secret nature reserves that he manages. A young woman living in a squat and eco-community shows me around the living spaces. A trustee of Bankside Open Spaces Trust unlocks the gates of Crossbones at twilight, we wander, and he shares his personal stories relating to the space. So many caretakers and custodians of special places, so many like-minded and curious wanderers, have been so kind, and so welcoming. Often, people are the gatekeepers to exploratory adventures, they offer you access to places that are "off-limits" in a sense, they make wanderings more exciting, more vibrant, and more real.

Being a guide has opened doors to many places I never thought to enter. I've taken groups to theatres to watch plays and musicals, to tourist sites like Wimbledon Tennis Museum. I've spent so much time in places I wouldn't normally, places like Notting Hill and Mayfair. I've been treated to so many meals by so many lovely guests. I've received invitations from people I've met to stay in their homes in places like Ghana and South Africa and Indonesia.

I've had the privilege, most importantly, to connect with and be part of so many extraordinary diverse communities.

Sometimes I close my eyes and I play back memories of places I've traversed and people I've met. Together they make up an extraordinary mosaic – I feel overwhelmed by the miracles, the sheer magic, and the beauty I've experienced. Each memory connects me to my calling. It reminds me of how blessed I am to live in a city like London and to be a guide. I remember traversing an ancient hilltop in a downpour, the sun comes out and a rainbow appears. I remember reading a book in the woods by Welsh Harp Reservoir one afternoon – the sense of peace and joy and freedom I felt wash over me. I remember having beans on toast in the café at the Age Reminiscent Centre in Blackheath. I remember wandering around the grounds of Strawberry Hill House one morning and listening to the waves at the beach by Gabriel's Wharf one night.

I remember gazing at the city skyline from One Tree Hill nature reserve, from the rooftop of the Bussey Building, and the Politics Department at Goldsmith's Warmington Tower. I remember listening to the ticking of hands at the Clock Makers Museum, filming from the treehouse at the Free-Range Garden. I remember midnight wanderings in Shoreditch, stargazing from Parliament Hill, counting the headlights from Archway's suicide bridge, hiking up to the snowy peak of Stave Hill in South London. I remember the empty velodrome and the empty palm court. I remember light and shadows dancing on water and on concrete. Our memories are invaluable and precious. They allow us to escape and to understand. A city offers you so many opportunities to heal, grow, and learn - to meet with spirit guides and to find the guide within.

I believe that everyone we meet on our life journey has something to tell us, to teach us, to give us, or to take away from us. Maybe we don't realise it at the time, but such connections are significant and require our attention, our awe even. The more you open yourself to the universe, the more you allow yourself to believe in the magic of new beginnings, in the possibility of change, in the faith that often lies dormant within us, waiting to stir – the more you will experience bursts of inspiration, clarity, and revelation.

Guiding has taught me so many lessons that I carry with me wherever I go. I have learnt to show up, to keep showing up, even when it is difficult. I have learnt that the journey matters more than the destination. I have learnt to keep going, whatever the weather. I have guided through blizzards and heatwaves and storms, the end brings about a greater joy, the more difficult the journey. I have learnt to be present, to be adaptable and resilient, and empathetic. I have learnt to have few expectations – to be humble and truthful and to do everything with love. I have learnt that we have a lot more in common than we'd like to think, even with those from whom we set ourselves apart. I've learnt that I belong to myself, and to others. We owe each other a lot. To love, to accept others as they are, to listen, to be kind even when it is difficult, to be patient, to realise the sanctity of human relations, to seek guidance, always with God – these are the things that I've learnt and continue to learn. The path before you is wide open.

Epilogue

"Life shrinks and expands in proportion to one's courage."— Anaïs Nin

The weather is beginning to change here in Lahore. The days are getting longer and brighter and warmer. Spring is almost here. When I first arrived, it was cold and dark, the nights were long and it felt like winter would never end. It's been a difficult journey, returning after so long, reconnecting with estranged loved ones, exploring the city, writing and thinking and thinking and thinking. It's been emotionally exhausting, but restorative. Everyone has been so kind, open-hearted and warm. I used to struggle to accept acts of kindness with grace and humility, but I don't anymore. I am grateful and express my gratitude, and I try to return blessings wherever I can.

We live in difficult times, the world is ridden with troubles – the bushlands are burning, the ice caps are melting, coronavirus is fast spreading. We've seen a rise in nationalist violence and unspeakable oppression rooted in fear, hatred and distrust. Racial, sexual, and economic inequality are rife, hunger and poverty are widespread. People are facing deep collective and individual loss. The world is in a state of malaise, and deep crisis.

It is so easy to lose hope in times like these, in fact, perhaps it feels natural. But we can't. What can we do on an individual and collective level? We can love each other enough to want better for each other, we can engage, we can listen, we can help, we can pray. To heal the world, we must first heal ourselves, heal our communities. We have to care for one another, as though it's the reason why we're here. We have to have compassion, to be accountable, to forgive more readily, and to have the humility to meet people where they are. To cultivate the desire to give more than we get and to feel content, whatever the outcome.

It's easy to feel powerless, to feel overcome and cynical - it takes strength to believe in goodness, to fight for justice, for equality, for change, in any small way we can. We have to find peace within, to embody peace, and to allow others to do the same. We have to work on giving less advice to others and focus more on addressing the lack within us. We have to do whatever we can to improve the situation we collectively find ourselves in.

In a few days, I will go back to London, and Lahore will once again feel like a dream. For the first time in years, my life feels wide open, and as frightening as that feels, it also feels exciting and liberating. There's always room to recreate ourselves and our lives for the better. It is when we find ourselves at loss, that we are closest to a breakthrough. I continue to believe in miracles and to believe in God. Wherever I find myself, whatever path presents itself before me, I pray I continue to remain a renegade guide in whatever form that may take.

March 2020

Acknowledgments

Six years ago I began working on a book called Living London. My intentions for writing the book were two-fold; to share the stories of the incredible places, communities, and individuals that make London such a unique and beautiful city, and to inspire others to find freedom and relief in everyday exploration. Many years, a thousand hidden spaces and 160,000 words later, I abandoned the project.

One day, I decided to write a personal essay on what being a guide meant to me. It marked the beginnings of my book *On Belonging, Reflections of a Renegade Guide*.

I never set out to write this book. It has been both a difficult and easy undertaking. Although I largely wrote it over a short period of time in Lahore, it took forever to acquire the insights, stories and experiences it holds. Even so, this book offers just a fleeting glimpse into some of the explorations and encounters that have marked my journey.

This book would not have been made possible without all the incredible and inspiring individuals and communities who let me into their worlds, who have shared their stories and wisdom with me. Some of the names have been changed to protect the privacy of certain individuals.

Thank you Lisa Rahman for your reassurance, support, kindness, and for designing my book cover. Thank you Aleesha Nandhra for your beautiful illustration. Thank you Jackee Holder for encouraging me to share my story. Thank you Sarah Khan for editing my book.

Thank you, Noreen, for always believing in me, supporting me, and showing me kindness - you are the most spirited woman I know. Thank you, Sofia, for continually inspiring me with your creativity, love, humour, and authenticity. Thank you, dad, for always encouraging me to explore and to write – and for being my greatest inspiration. Thank you mum, for your patience and love, and for teaching me the meaning of selflessness. Thank you to my brothers for accepting me as I am.

Thank you to the special souls who I have not mentioned in this book. You will always be close to my heart.

Thank you to my aunts, uncles, and cousins in Lahore for the kindness you've shown me.

Thank you to Imogen and Imran for working with me, continually inspiring me, and believing in what I do.

Thank you to my magical friends, flitters, teachers, and mentors who have inspired and wandered with me.

Thank you to everyone who has come along to a wandering tour. I feel so privileged and blessed to have met you.

Most of all, thank you God - Allah – for always Guiding me back to You.

Links

For wandering tours, workshops, commissions, and projects visit the Living London website: **www.livinglondon.org** and for hundreds of hidden London gems and stories click 'blog' on the link above.

Discover the magic of everyday exploration on social media.

Find me **@livinglon**

Contact Email: **saira_niazi@hotmail.co.uk**

Printed in Poland
by Amazon Fulfillment
Poland Sp. z o.o., Wrocław